Alec Wilder

Philip Lambert

UNIVERSITY OF ILLINOIS PRESS
Urbana, Chicago, and Springfield

Manufactured in the
United States of America
1 2 3 4 5 C P 5 4 3 2 1
This book is printed
on acid-free paper.

Library of Congress Cataloging-in-Publication Data
Lambert, Philip, 1958–
Alec Wilder / by Philip Lambert.
p. cm. — (American composers)
Includes bibliographical references and index.
ISBN 978-0-252-03760-3 (hardcover : alk. paper) —
ISBN 978-0-252-07913-9 (pbk. : alk. paper) —
ISBN 978-0-252-09484-2 (e-book)
1. Wilder, Alec. 2. Composers—United States—Biography.
I. Title.
ML410.W6975L36 2013
780.92—dc23 2012036291
[B]

ALEC WILDER

AMERICAN

Composers

A list of books in the series appears at the end of this book.

To the memory of
my father-in-law,
Ben Taublieb,
and
my mother,
Joanne Lambert Todd

CONTENTS

PREFACE

ALEC WILDER (1907–80) WAS A MAN of diverse renown. Sophisticated audiophiles in the early 1940s knew him as the composer of a highly original series of octets that deftly melded jazz, pop, and classical traditions. Musicians and producers in the New York recording industry in the 1940s and '50s knew him as a talented arranger and orchestrator. To legions of children and their parents during that time, he was the creative mind behind some of the happy sounds playing over and over on the phonograph. Mabel Mercer, Tony Bennett, Peggy Lee, and many other recording artists in the middle decades of the twentieth century knew him primarily as a gifted songwriter. The filmmaker Jerome Hill knew him as a composer of movie music. In the late 1950s through the 1970s, Wilder was especially known as a composer of chamber music for every instrument and concert music for large ensembles. Meanwhile, he was also writing a trailblazing book and cohosting a radio series on the subject of the American popular song in the first half of the twentieth century. Throughout his life, to musicians across the professional spectrum, including the likes of Mitch Miller, John Barrows, Harvey Phillips, and Marian McPartland, he was known as an eccentric visitor, composer-on-demand, poet, prolific correspondent, and loyal friend.

He was also a bit of a mystery. With talents that could not be exclusively claimed by either the jazz or classical communities, he was never fully embraced by either. He avoided the limelight and was unknown to the general public for most of his life. He often wrote music as gifts for friends, without keeping a copy for himself, and he may not have known whether his work was ever performed. People wondered: What inspired him? What were the roots of his unique gifts? Was he a visionary? Dilettante? Lovable eccentric? Tortured genius? Often the question was simply: Where is he? He had no true permanent residence throughout his adult life, just an informal arrangement with the Algonquin Hotel in New

York City, and he could disappear on a moment's notice into a compartment of a passenger train destined for parts unknown.

Fortunately, he had friends and admirers who have sought to tie together some of the diverse strands of his life and career. Aware that Wilder's instrumental scores were scattered among offices and studios and piano benches around the country and largely unavailable to performers, the tubist Harvey Phillips first began to collect and organize Wilder's music in 1964. The publishing catalog and inventory eventually shifted to Gunther Schuller's Margun Music publishing company in 1976, more recently to Schirmer and Hal Leonard. The vocal-music scores mostly remained in the offices of the Richmond Organization (TRO) in New York, thanks to the support and generosity of Howard Richmond and Al Brackman, and the diligent stewardship of Judith Bell. Meanwhile, manuscripts, letters, poems, and other documents that had somehow survived Wilder's nomadic existence—mostly because friends such as William Engvick and James Sibley Watson Jr. had never thrown anything away—found a home at the Alec Wilder Archive of the Sibley Music Library at the Eastman School of Music in Wilder's hometown of Rochester, New York. Eastman also helped bring Wilder's achievements more into the public consciousness, awarding him an honorary doctorate in 1973 and dedicating the Alec Wilder Reading Room of its newly built library building in 1991. Recognition also came with a posthumous election to the Songwriters Hall of Fame in 1983, and with annual concerts of the Friends of Alec Wilder in New York, which continue to this day.

Important publications about Wilder's life and work began to appear in 1991, in the form of an especially informative publishers' catalog from Margun Music, followed by David Demsey and Ronald Prather's comprehensive bio-bibliography published by Greenwood Press in 1993, a valuable snapshot of the state of Wilder research at that time. The definitive biography of Wilder, Desmond Stone's *Alec Wilder in Spite of Himself*, appeared from Oxford University Press in 1996. Drawing from extensive personal interviews and close access to primary documents, Stone revealed copious details of Wilder's life, including revelations about his alcoholism (and his reputation for abrasive behavior while intoxicated), sexuality (he claimed to be heterosexual but may have had homosexual relationships), and parenthood (he apparently fathered a daughter with a woman he saw often early in his adulthood, although in later life he maintained no relationship with her or the child). On the Internet, an Alec Wilder group has flourished on Yahoo.com, and wilderworld.podomatic.com helped celebrated the Wilder centennial in 2007 by inaugurating a series of podcasts of Wilder's music, including both well-known recordings and rare ones. A good many of Wilder's scores are now available for rental or purchase, and new song collections and recordings continue to appear. He is not the shadowy figure he once was.

The mysteries that remain mostly concern the nature of his art. One primary goal of this book is to give closer consideration to Alec Wilder's music—to consider not only the biographical circumstances of his creative pursuits but also the historical context of his basic musical language, his artistic debts and influences. In Wilder's case, this often means focusing on the nature of musical style and how traditional conceptions of style may or may not apply. It also means paying close attention to particular compositional techniques as they arise and evolve. The trends that emerge take their place in an overall narrative that is essentially chronological, in separate chapters roughly corresponding to the decades of the Christian calendar, following Wilder's personal and artistic growth from childhood through maturity. A final chapter offers a general perspective on the composer and his work. Seemingly disparate musical and biographical threads ultimately weave together into a complete fabric.

A NOTE ON SOURCES

THIS BOOK HAS THREE APPENDICES. "Selected Works" compiles essential information about Wilder's work to support and supplement the main text. Full citations for major writings by and about Alec Wilder are given in "For Further Reading," and major recordings are listed in "Suggested Listening." Many other important sources, including monographs, articles, and recordings, are fully cited in the endnotes.

References to the three primary collections of unpublished Wilder-related material may appear in the main text or endnotes as follows:

Wilder Archive The Alec Wilder Archive at the Sibley Music Library, Eastman School of Music, Rochester, N.Y.

TRO Archive The extensive collection of original manuscripts, reproductions, and published scores, mostly of songs and other vocal music, kept in the offices of the Richmond Organization (TRO) in New York.

Wilder Papers Two boxes of letters, clippings, and other documents, held by the New York Public Library Primary Research Division (catalogued as "Alec Wilder Papers, 1939–2000").

References to, and quotations from, Wilder's writings may be cited in brief within the text or endnotes as follows:

"The Tuxedo" Wilder's first attempt at an autobiographical essay in the early 1960s, surviving as a typescript of about sixty pages, with pencil corrections (Wilder Archive 5–2, box 2, folder 8).

The Search A much more expansive memoir handwritten in 1970 on 171 pages of two spiral notebooks (Wilder Archive 5–2, box 1, folder 15).

Life Story The final version of Wilder's memoir, written in 1971 and 1972 and surviving as a 189-page typescript, with pencil corrections (Wilder Archive 6–1, box 1, folder 1).

American Popular Song Wilder's major treatise on popular song in America in the first half of the twentieth century, published in 1972 (full citation in "For Further Reading").

Letters I Never Mailed An autobiography in the form of personal letters, first published in 1975 (full citation in "For Further Reading"). Page references are to the 2005 edition.

Elegant Refuge A never-published memoir written in 1976 about Wilder's experiences at his only real "home," the Algonquin Hotel in New York, surviving as a 250-page typescript, with pencil corrections (Wilder Archive 5–2, box 1, folders 5 and 6).

Songs Were Made to Sing The third edition of the Wilder popular-song collection, published by TRO-Ludlow in 1976, which includes Wilder's verbal preambles to many of the songs, providing valuable historical and biographical context.

ACKNOWLEDGMENTS

MORE THAN THIRTY YEARS AFTER Alec Wilder's death, the community of Wilder friends, fans, and advocates is still going strong. This first became apparent to me at the beginning of my research for this book, when I contacted Bob Levy, and he put me in touch with a network of Wilder enthusiasts who were eager to help in any way they could. I thank Bob for his passion and generosity. He is more than a Wilder expert and valuable resource; he is also an inspiration.

Among the happy consequences of Bob's assistance was the chance to know a key member of the network, a remarkable woman named Judy Bell, who is creative director of the Richmond Organization in New York. With an encyclopedic knowledge of all things Wilder, Judy was an endless source of crucial information for this book. More importantly, she allowed me unrestricted access to TRO's extensive collection of Wilder manuscripts, mostly the hundreds of songs and other vocal music. She also shared recordings and other arcana. I thank her for her generous, authoritative assistance and support. This book would not have been possible without her help.

I also gratefully acknowledge other members of the Wilder community who offered valuable advice and perspectives, including David Demsey, Rob Geller, Tom Hampson, Helen Ouzer, William R. Ploss, and Ronald Prather. I benefited enormously from their willingness to answer queries and share opinions.

Another vital part of the research for this book was the time I spent at the Wilder Archive in Rochester in August 2010. This was an enriching experience, not only because the holdings there are so extensive and beautifully preserved, but also because the staff members of the Sibley Music Library are so competent and accommodating. I thank David Peter Coppen for his able assistance, both when I was on site and in response to numerous subsequent followup inquiries and requests, and his assistant Matthew Colbert.

Back downstate, I acknowledge Bob Kosovsky and the staff at the New York Public Library for the Performing Arts at Lincoln Center; Thomas Lannon and Amanda Siegel at the main branch; and the librarians and interlibrary loan staff at the Newman Library of Baruch College, City University of New York.

I am also grateful to the Research Foundation of the City University of New York for funding in support of travel and other expenses. At the University of Illinois Press, I thank Laurie Matheson for her oversight of this project since its inception, and Tad Ringo and Matt Mitchell for their capable assistance with production and copyediting.

Saving the best for last, I thank my co-residents in the sorority house we call home: my wife Diane and our daughters Alice and Charlotte. They make everything and anything possible.

As I was nearing completion of this book, our family lost two of its most beloved, influential figures. My father-in-law, Ben Taublieb, was a war veteran and pillar of the community whose daily life epitomized hard work and devotion to family. My mother, Joanne Lambert Todd, was an educator and businesswoman whose personal warmth and irrepressible spirit touched everyone she met. I dedicate this book to their memory, hoping that anything valuable in its pages will stand as evidence of their impact and legacy.

Made in USA. All Rights Reserved Including Public Performance for Profit. Used by Permission.

I FELT A FUNERAL, words by Emily Dickinson; music by Alec Wilder, TRO-© Copyright 2012, Ludlow Music, Inc., New York. International Copyright Secured. Made in USA. All Rights Reserved Including Public Performance for Profit. Used by Permission.

I'LL BE AROUND, words and music by Alec Wilder, TRO-© Copyright 1942 (Renewed), Ludlow Music, Inc., New York. International Copyright Secured. Made in USA. All Rights Reserved Including Public Performance for Profit. Used by Permission.

JACK, THIS IS MY HUSBAND, by Alec Wilder, TRO-© Copyright 1947 (Renewed), Ludlow Music, Inc., New York. International Copyright Secured. Made in USA. All Rights Reserved Including Public Performance for Profit. Used by Permission.

SERENADE FROM JAZZ SUITE FOR HORN QUARTET, by Alec Wilder, TRO-© Copyright 1962 (Renewed), Ludlow Music, Inc., New York. International Copyright Secured. Made in USA. All Rights Reserved Including Public Performance for Profit. Used by Permission.

JUST ONE, words and music by Alec Wilder, TRO-© Copyright 2012, Ludlow Music, Inc., New York. International Copyright Secured. Made in USA. All Rights Reserved Including Public Performance for Profit. Used by Permission.

LISTEN TO YOUR HEART, from "Pinocchio," words by William Engvick; music by Alec Wilder, TRO-© Copyright 1957 (Renewed), Ludlow Music, Inc., New York. International Copyright Secured. Made in USA. All Rights Reserved Including Public Performance for Profit. Used by Permission.

NEUROTIC GOLDFISH, by Alec Wilder, TRO-© Copyright 1942 (Renewed), Ludlow Music, Inc., New York. International Copyright Secured. Made in USA. All Rights Reserved Including Public Performance for Profit. Used by Permission.

NIGHT TALK, words and music by Alec Wilder, TRO-© Copyright 1968 (Renewed), Ludlow Music, Inc., New York. International Copyright Secured. Made in USA. All Rights Reserved Including Public Performance for Profit. Used by Permission.

ONCE IN A MILLION YEARS, words and music by Alec Wilder, TRO-© Copyright 2012, Ludlow Music, Inc., New York. International Copyright Secured. Made in USA. All Rights Reserved Including Public Performance for Profit. Used by Permission.

SOUTH—TO A WARMER PLACE, words by Loonis McGlohon, music

by Alec Wilder, TRO-© Copyright 1981 and 1982, Ludlow Music, Inc., New York, and Warner-Tamerlane Publishing Corp., Los Angeles, CA. International Copyright Secured. Made in USA. All Rights Reserved Including Public Performance for Profit. Used by Permission.

A LONG NIGHT, words by Rogers Brackett, music by Alec Wilder, TRO-© Copyright 1976 (Renewed), Ludlow Music, Inc., New York, and Warner-Tamerlane Publishing Corp., Los Angeles, CA. International Copyright Secured. Made in USA. All Rights Reserved Including Public Performance for Profit. Used by Permission.

THE IDIOT, music by Alec Wilder, TRO-© Copyright 2012, Ludlow Music, Inc., New York. International Copyright Secured. Made in USA. All Rights Reserved Including Public Performance for Profit. Used by Permission.

THE WINTER OF MY DISCONTENT, words by Ben Ross Berenberg, music by Alec Wilder, TRO-© Copyright 2012, Ludlow Music, Inc., New York, and Warner-Tamerlane Publishing Corp., Los Angeles, CA. International Copyright Secured. Made in USA. All Rights Reserved Including Public Performance for Profit. Used by Permission.

THEME AND VARIATIONS, by Alec Wilder, TRO-© Copyright 1953 (Renewed), Ludlow Music, Inc., New York. International Copyright Secured. Made in USA. All Rights Reserved Including Public Performance for Profit. Used by Permission.

WHAT HAPPENED LAST NIGHT? by Alec Wilder, TRO-© Copyright 1957 (Renewed), Ludlow Music, Inc., New York. International Copyright Secured. Made in USA. All Rights Reserved Including Public Performance for Profit. Used by Permission.

WHEN YESTERDAY I LOVED YOU, words by Loonis McGlohon, music by Alec Wilder, TRO-© Copyright 2009, Ludlow Music, Inc., New York. International Copyright Secured. Made in USA. All Rights Reserved Including Public Performance for Profit. Used by Permission.

WHERE DO YOU GO? words by Arnold Sundgaard, music by Alec Wilder, TRO-© Copyright 1959 (Renewed), Ludlow Music, Inc., New York, and Hampshire House Publishing Corp., New York. International Copyright Secured. Made in USA. All Rights Reserved Including Public Performance for Profit. Used by Permission.

WHERE'S THAT HEARTACHE? words by Loonis McGlohon, music by Alec Wilder, TRO-© Copyright 1990, Ludlow Music, Inc., New York. International Copyright Secured. Made in USA. All Rights Reserved Including Public Performance for Profit. Used by Permission.

WHILE WE'RE YOUNG, words by William Engvick, music by Morty Palitz and Alec Wilder, TRO-© Copyright 1943 (Renewed), 1944 (Renewed), Ludlow Music, Inc., New York. International Copyright Secured. Made in USA. All Rights Reserved Including Public Performance for Profit. Used by Permission.

WHO CAN I TURN TO? words and music by Alec Wilder and William Engvick, TRO-© Copyright 1941 (Renewed), Ludlow Music, Inc., New York. International Copyright Secured. Made in USA. All Rights Reserved Including Public Performance for Profit. Used by Permission.

WOODWIND QUINTET NO. **2**, by Alec Wilder, TRO-© Copyright 2005, Ludlow Music, Inc., New York. International Copyright Secured. Made in USA. All Rights Reserved Including Public Performance for Profit. Used by Permission.

1 Awakenings

Musical Experiences through the Early 1930s

FROM THE MOMENT OF HIS BIRTH, on February 16, 1907, in Rochester, New York, Alexander Wilder was a child of privilege. His father's family were prominent local bankers. His mother's family, descended from the Chews of New Orleans, had similarly prospered at the First National Bank of nearby Geneva. His full name, Alexander Lafayette Chew Wilder, sustained a legacy from his mother's father, Alexander Lafayette Chew, whose godfather was the Marquis de Lafayette. Writing about his early life years later, Wilder recalled a childhood of comfort and affluence in a large house well stocked with material possessions and maintained by servants, alongside an older brother and sister.[1] He did not, however, remember a warm, nurturing home. After his father's sudden death in 1909, his mother was ill-equipped to manage the household alone and descended into alcoholism and depression. The baby of the family, who was known as "Alexander" or "Alex," not yet "Alec," developed an orientation toward domestic instability that he would carry with him throughout his life.

Music held a rather ordinary presence in Wilder's youth. He recalls witnessing a shaky piano performance by his Aunt Emma of "The Whistler and His Dog," a tune made famous by Arthur Pryor's band and published in sheet music in 1905. In his memoirs he also mentions records playing on the Victrola in his house, including "Esmeralda" (perhaps an arrangement of Cesare Pugni's ballet music of 1844) and "Dark Town Strutter's Ball," in the 1917 recording by a saxophone sextet, Six Brown Brothers. His sister, he recalls, sang popular songs such as "The Girl on the Magazine Cover" (Irving Berlin, from *Stop! Look! Listen!* [1915]) and "Wait till the Cows Come Home" (Ivan Caryll and Anne Caldwell, from *Jack o'Lantern* [1917]), showing special affection for tunes from the currently hot songwriting team of Jerome Kern and P. G. Wodehouse, including "My Castle in the Air" (*Miss Springtime* [1916]), "The Crickets Are Calling" (*Leave It to Jane* [1917]), and "And I Am All Alone" (*Have a Heart* [1917]).[2] But young Alexander did not harbor a particular affinity for music and did not study or perform music in any formal way during his childhood. He was given freedom and independence, and he spent much of his time alone, with books and fantasies.

After Wilder attended private schools for a few years in Rochester, his family moved downstate in pursuit of broader educational opportunities. For the family's youngest, however, a year at St. Paul's School in Garden City, Long Island, and a few months at the Lawrenceville School in New Jersey brought only frustration and distress. A sensitive soul with relatively esoteric interests, he was unable to feel comfortable with earthier, more athletically inclined classmates. He was bullied and harassed. He finally found solace at the Collegiate School on the Upper West Side of Manhattan, where he met kindred spirits and flourished in a nurturing academic environment. He was well-liked and active, a member of the debate team and glee club, and he graduated in 1924 as "Most Likely to Succeed."

But succeed at what? He had failed his regents exams, New York's barometer of college preparedness, and was not destined for a traditional postsecondary education. He had no clearly defined career goals. For more than a year after finishing high school, he thought of being a writer and labored over poems and stories, finally deciding that he had "learned a lot about writing" but "didn't know what to write about" (*Life Story*, 17). He had a brief flirtation with an acting school. Mostly he and his friends Carroll Dunn, whom he had met at the Jersey Shore a few summers earlier, and Lavinia Faxon enjoyed lives of leisure, in day trips up the Hudson and longwinded discussions over late-night dinners. Wilder recalled, "Those were the innocent twenties with their romantic speakeasies, their flappers, their laughter, and their benign ignorance of what the world really was. Oh, those long, intense discussions late at night in Chinese restaurants drinking tea and eating almond cakes, for the speakeasies didn't reach us until later. Our probably corny foolishness, our love of poetry and arrogant and naive speculations about life, life, life!!" (*Life Story*, 23).

His decision to pursue a career in music came in 1925 or early 1926, following a passion that had been growing for some time. During one recent summer vacation he had taken up the banjo and had learned to play well enough to be hired for dances and welcomed into local bar bands at the Jersey Shore. He had also begun teaching himself to play the piano and read staff notation. He had amassed a collection of popular sheet music and had made a few attempts at writing songs of his own. A turning point in his musical ambitions, he believed, came during travels in Italy with his father's sister, Clara Haushalter, in the summer of 1924, just after graduation from Collegiate. During this trip, he later wrote, he "must have decided to become a composer" (*Life Story*, 21). While in Italy, he rented a piano and worked through piano reductions of Wagner scores. He wrote an "innocuous little piano piece." The countryside, and the attentions of a sweet Italian girl, had inspired him. Subsequently, during his postgraduation sabbatical back in New York, he followed Carroll Dunn's advice to "try something more ambitious than songs" and wrote what he called a "tone poem" for piano and then a choral setting of a Kipling poem that Dunn had given him.

These were the musical experiences he brought with him, along with a desire to get away from his family in New York City, when he decided to return to Rochester in 1926, seeking enlightenment in the elegant halls of a relatively new institute for serious musical study.

At Eastman

The Eastman School of Music of the University of Rochester had been established five years earlier, on a twelve-million-dollar bequest from George Eastman, the founder of the city's signature corporation, Eastman Kodak. Since 1924, the school's director had been Howard Hanson, already celebrated as an educator and administrator and just back from three years of study in Rome as a recipient of the Rome Prize for his ballet *California Forest Play of 1920*. Wilder's arrival at Eastman in 1926 reflected a certain commitment toward a future in music, even if the exact direction and dimensions of that career path remained hazily drawn. Up until that time he had only dabbled, and he was hardly confident that a professional music school was the right place for him, or that he would even be welcomed into such a community. But he was self-aware enough to trust his instincts, and he had the financial wherewithal to pursue a blossoming passion. He became a familiar figure in Eastman's main hall and in coffee shops and speakeasies of the surrounding neighborhood in the late 1920s, known for eccentric behavior and attire and for generous financial gifts to Eastman students. A sizable inheritance from his father, which was officially released into his custody at age twenty-one in 1928, sustained him for several years, eventually extending into the bleakest days of the Great Depression.

Wilder was a presence at Eastman during that time, but he was never formally enrolled as a student. He never applied or auditioned. He simply appeared at the office door of a faculty member, Herbert Inch, seeking an opinion on his choral setting of the Kipling poem that Carroll Dunn had given him. As Wilder later explained, Inch "kindly suggested study" (*The Search*, 39). Wilder took private counterpoint lessons with Inch for several semesters starting in 1926, studying Bach and writing model compositions. It proved to be a formative experience in his musical development, breeding a belief that "counterpoint is the bones of music. Harmony and rhythm are fascinating, but to me they represent flesh as opposed to bone. And without the strength of interdependent lines, the musical building may collapse" (*Letters I Never Mailed*, 84). Wilder came to regard Bach as "the greatest genius of them all" (*Letters I've Never Mailed*, 86) and "the high point of Western civilization" (*Life Story*, 33). Not just a linear orientation but actual contrapuntal techniques such as fugue and canon would become vital elements of the concert music Wilder would later compose.

He had a less fulfilling experience with another Eastman professor, Edward Royce, the son of the renowned Harvard philosopher Josiah Royce. In a series of private composition lessons, Royce attempted to impart a working method grounded in logic and order. "Everything must be foursquare," Wilder recalled. "I certainly am all for order and discipline, but Mr. Royce had me almost in a musical straitjacket" (*Letters I Never Mailed*, 85). Wilder does not explain the full details of Royce's system, offering only general accounts of methods that seem to rely more on planning and technical organization than on instinct or spontaneity. With Royce he also studied Beethoven piano sonatas, apparently with an emphasis on the intellectual basis of compositional decisions. Wilder wrote that he respected Beethoven's "orderly mind" but that he was "not nearly so enthusiastic about his music as Mr. Royce would like me to be" (*Letters I've Never Mailed*, 86).

Wilder's reaction against the hyperrationality of Royce's approach and Beethoven's music might initially seem to be at odds with his high regard for Inch's tutelage and the constructive complexity of Bach's counterpoint. But Wilder is simply making a familiar distinction between strict and free composition. He places high value on the "strict" contrapuntal skill required to produce canons and fugues, but he also believes that "free" treatment of motives and themes is just as valid. In his writings, he praises composers whom he believes embody creative freedom, even if he has to apologize for it: "Forgive the sacrilege (since they employ little or no counterpoint), but I admit to great affection for Debussy and Ravel—particularly the Debussy string quartet, Ravel's *Daphnis and Chloé*, and what I've heard on records of Debussy's *Pelléas and Mélisande*" (*Letters I Never Mailed*, 86). He can value the craftsmanship of Bach while also responding to the "sentimental, unaggressive nature" of Debussy (*Life Story*, 33). There is room for both, as Wilder would go on to demonstrate, time and time again, in his own musical creations of the decades to come.

Wilder wrote some short piano pieces for Royce but did not continue with an extended course of study. He also attended some of Howard Hanson's classes without any formal arrangement. Mostly he set out on his own, absorbing the sounds he heard in performances by Eastman students and faculty. He learned orchestration not from a class but from private study of Cecil Forsyth's manual.[3] And he began to write music of all sorts—short pieces for flute and for cello, settings of poetry by James Stephens and Edgar Allan Poe.

Eventually, during his first years at Eastman, Wilder wrote music of sufficient distinction to be programmed on some of the American Composers Concerts, a series started by Hanson in 1925 to promote new young talent. In the 1927–28 season, only his second year at the school, six of Wilder's songs for voice and orchestra appeared on one of the concerts, and a program from the following year included Wilder's new tone poem, *Symphonic Piece*.[4] That his music fails to appear on similar programs in subsequent years may be a result of Wilder's mishandling of the latter premiere. At one of the rehearsals of the work, it became clear that Wilder had made errors in scoring the trumpets and horns, and Hanson had gone in and fixed them. Distressed and embarrassed about his mistakes, Wilder declined to be in the audience for the performance and receive Hanson's acknowledgment, opting instead for an alcoholic haze at a nearby speakeasy. It was, Wilder wrote, "the night I lost Dr. Hanson."[5]

Upstate, Downstate

Wilder was a regular presence at Eastman between 1926 and 1929 or 1930. He blended in with the academic life and developed close friendships that would last for decades, with students such as Mitchell Miller (studying oboe, long before television singalongs), Frank Baker (studying voice), Joe Schiff (viola), Frances Alexander (later Mrs. Mitchell Miller, piano), Jimmy Caruana (clarinet), and the French hornists John Barrows, Jimmy Buffington, and Sam Richlin. Through Joe

Schiff he met another lifelong friend, the photographer Louis Ouzer. In the early 1930s, with the country in economic crisis, Rochester continued to be Wilder's base, but he surrendered more and more to a restless urge for mobility and changing scenery. He began a love affair with train travel that he would maintain for the rest of his life, an impulse to depart on a moment's notice for far-flung destinations, with no or very little purpose. Wilder explained:

> Music was the constant factor, the dominating compulsion, but never to the exclusion of my love for railroads, of reading or of spending time in strange communities. I say "strange" because, in spite of my love for a few people, I still preferred to spend most of my time alone, and I was happier in towns where I knew nobody, had no fear of the phone ringing, no threat of appointments or dinner dates.
>
> So I went to Abington [Massachusetts], Virginia, Charleston, New Orleans, Chicago, St. Petersburg, and countless villages whose names I've forgotten. But they had one trait in common: they all must be reachable by railroad. I disliked entering a town or city by automobile. Railroads to this day make a romantic mystery of travel. (*The Search,* 73)

He was especially drawn back downstate via the Empire State Express, which ran frequently between central Rochester and Manhattan's Pennsylvania Station, along the banks of the Erie Canal and Hudson River.

Wherever he found himself, he continued to write music, building on his experiences at Eastman. He wrote many more art songs, filling manuscript books with earnest efforts in search of a distinctive compositional voice. Many of these survive in what have been designated the Wilder "songbooks" (see "Selected Works," section I). They include musical settings of a variety of poetic voices, from the classic (John Keats) to the recent and conventional (James Stephens) to the deeply introspective (Emily Dickinson). They also cover a wide musical terrain, some aspiring toward a simple elegance ("Nancy Walsh," "Autumn Chant," "Wild Swans"), others pushing boundaries of dissonance and style ("I Hide Myself," "I Felt a Funeral"). Some of the poems he chose are multi-stanza "epics" ("Annabelle Lee," "The Fifteen Acres"), but he more often chose shorter poems and wrote music to match the poetic focus and intensity. Harmonically the songs are lush and colorful, many showing the influence of Debussy, although some sound more like Satie ("Song, I Am Tired to Death"), and others capture an ethnic or folk quality of the original poem ("Besides That"). Generally speaking, the songs have many original moments, often betraying a sensibility that veers away from the boundaries of a conventional "art song" and borrows liberally from popular traditions. Even in his earliest efforts at musical composition, Wilder employed ideas and adopted attitudes that would become his trademark.

He seems to have responded to Emily Dickinson with particular ardor, and his settings of eight of her poems in Songbook B are among the most musically inventive of these early works. "I Felt a Funeral," for example, begins with thick, dissonant harmonies changing on each downbeat, like the tolling of distant bells on a dark night, or the pacing of a motley funeral procession (Example 1). Some of the chords are recognizable tonal structures—the G♭ major triad at "brain" especially stands out—but most consist of clustered dissonances, often bringing together notes of a whole-tone scale. The vocal line snakes upward to the climactic phrase "sense is breaking through," usually doubling notes from within the piano chords. But the melody itself is hardly the primary focus; the central idea of the song is the sound of the piano's chords with the interweaving melody.

Example 1: "I Felt a Funeral," mm. 1–17

What seems to have captured Wilder's interest most intensely is the challenge of creating a novel, expressive progression of harmonies. This would become a familiar motivation in much of his later work.

Wilder does not say whether he heard any of these early songs performed. He may have had them in mind when he later recalled "all those concert songs I've never heard sung" (*The Search*, 166). But some of them might have been given informal readings by friends (such as Frank Baker and Frances Alexander); at least eight were copied out separately in ink, as if to provide scores for performers.[6] Performance prospects or not, he continued to write. His series of art songs essentially represents a compositional laboratory, the work of a creative artist teaching himself to compose, as he had earlier taught himself to play banjo and piano. In similar fashion, he wrote a cello concerto for the principal cellist of the Rochester Philharmonic, George Finckel, who "never got around to even trying it out" (*Life Story*, 54).[7] Wilder does remember hearing a reading by Finckel of some "short cello pieces" and a performance in nearby Geneva of a piece for cello and harp (*Life Story*, 54). Mitch Miller has recalled playing a new piece by Wilder on his graduation recital in 1932.[8] While the scores for these works have not surfaced and may have been discarded, score and parts do survive for a five-movement string quartet dating from this era, an ambitious blending of stern contrapuntal passages, dense motivic development, and jazzy, syncopated rhythms.[9] Wilder later described this work as a "bumbling burst of joy over having discovered the marvel of music but with no technique or sense of direction to guide my hand" (*Letters I Never Mailed*, 100). He remembers showing scores of his string quartet and cello concerto to Aaron Copland (*Letters I Never Mailed*, 100–101, 113–15). (Wilder recalls Copland's reaction: "You said I was more interesting than my music.") Years later, Wilder told Whitney Balliett that he had found a notice about a possible performance of the string quartet in his mother's purse after she died, in 1932.[10]

At some point during these years in Rochester, he made the acquaintance of James Sibley Watson Jr., a wealthy nonpracticing physician who was the co-owner and publisher of the progressive literary magazine *The Dial* from 1919 to 1929, and who had recently begun to make avant-garde films.[11] Their meeting came about after an odd encounter in the Eastman main hall:

> A rather shrewd-looking, countrified man sidled up to me and asked me if I'd like to appear in a movie. I had heard that an experimental film had been made up on Prince Street in Dr. Watson's father's farm-garage and that it had made considerable noise. It had been a version of *The Fall of the House of Usher.*
>
> This "movie scout" turned out to be a local painter by the name of Remson Wood who

> had begun to work with Dr. Watson on a new somewhat sex-riddled film about a butler who becomes sexually obsessed with a maid who has been temporarily lured to serve at a large dinner party.
>
> I looked, according to Mr. Wood, like a horny butler. Would I like to come up to the barn and try out for the role?
>
> This meant my meeting the great man, so naturally I agreed (though I knew nothing about acting or sex and was uninterested in both forms of exercise).
>
> I was hired, forced to shave off my mustache (a traumatic experience), work was done on the film, but it was never finished. (*The Search,* 53–54)

Eventually the team did complete new films, a brief sound-film spoof called *It Never Happened/Tomato's Another Day* (1930) and *Lot in Sodom* (1933), an adaptation of the Genesis story of Sodom and Gomorrah. Wilder became a part of the production team, eagerly sympathetic to the spirit of freedom and innovation of a group of progressive thinkers. He also attempted to write a score for Watson's earlier film, *The Fall of the House of Usher*, although these efforts fell short; many years later, he would write a new soundtrack that would work much better. Most importantly, through this experience Wilder found in James Sibley Watson a lifelong correspondent, confidante, financial supporter, and father figure. In the coming decades—Watson died two years after Wilder, in 1982—Wilder would write Watson hundreds of letters, many of them personal, soul-searching confessionals, often including earnest poetry. His letters to Watson could serve any purpose, from travel reportage to cathartic therapy to autobiographical sketching. They portray the inner Alec Wilder—a sensitive, introspective, often troubled artist whose constant search for relevance struggled valiantly against perceived threats and evils in modern society.[12]

But there is a whole other dimension to Wilder's life and musical development in the early 1930s. Amid contrapuntal studies and song settings and film projects and impromptu train trips, he was gaining a foothold as a writer of popular songs. On one of his trips downstate he had met Eddie Brandt, a singer–piano player in a speakeasy on the East Side of Manhattan. Brandt wrote pop tunes but needed a lyricist, and Wilder signed on because he was "so eager to become part of the song world" (*Elegant Refuge*, 22). Wilder wrote lyrics with titles like "Yes, Today? No, Yesterday!" and "Life's Just Funny That Way," and he and his partner made the rounds of New York publishers hawking their wares. One of their songs, "Day after Day," was actually published but then "just laid there like a dog in summer" (*Letters I Never Mailed*, 108). Eventually, however, their persistence paid off. They left a tin record of one of their songs for the Broadway star Marion Harris outside the stage door of the revue *The Second Little Show* in September or October of 1930.[13] Around that time, the songwriters for that show, Arthur Schwartz and Howard Dietz, were developing another revue, a feature for Fred Allen, Clifton Webb, and Libby Holman (who also starred in their revue *Little Show* a year earlier). When the new show, *Three's a Crowd*, premiered at the Selwyn Theater on October 15, 1930, the score included the Brandt-Wilder song "All the King's Horses"—presumably the song on the tin record. The show was a critical and commercial success and played for 271 performances, until June 6, 1931. In his appreciative review in the *New York Times* (October 16, 1930), Brooks Atkinson singled out the Brandt-Wilder number: "Among other assistants to the three stars is Margaret Lee, whose Tom Thumb caroling of a syncopated torch song, 'All the King's Horses,' deserves a word or two for itself, which it hereby gets."

The song, and the team, were short-lived. Wilder recalls that a recording of a completely different song with a similar title emerged at about the same time: "Our song . . . was well on the way to becoming a hit when, unfortunately, a song appeared from England called 'The King's Horses' which, thanks to Rudy Vallee's enthusiasm for it, wiped ours out" (*Elegant Refuge*, 22). But also, Wilder wanted to be more than a lyricist. He felt that his studies and experiences at Eastman had prepared him to write not just art songs and string quartets but also pop-style melodies and harmonies. He and Brandt drifted apart. Serving as his own lyricist, Wilder began devoting more and more energy to the craft of popular songwriting, often imagining how his creations would sound in the voices of specific performers such as Mildred Bailey, Ethel Waters, and Bing Crosby. He became as comfortable with popular idioms as he was with the sounds he had studied at Eastman. He moved easily back and forth between them, just as he did between a concert hall and a speakeasy.

Wilder's reputation for songwriting and wit gave rise to one of his last musical adventures while he still considered Rochester his home base, in April 1933. Cajoled by a group of mischievous students, he wrote script, music, and lyrics for an irreverent musical revue, *Haywire*, that was performed at the school by a cast of undergraduates. The show included a song about a marriage proposal, "Howd'ya Like My Name on Your Tombstone?" and a sendup of the American Composers Concerts, with a conductor mimicking the flailing arms of Howard Hanson.[14] Wilder later admitted that he also borrowed, without attribution, two of Eddie Brandt's tunes for the show, a trio for girls ("Wastin' My Time") and the closing number ("Here Today") (*Letters I Never Mailed*, 109–10). The show was a huge success in its two performances and earned special attention from one audience member, Leopold Mannes, who was in town to meet with his co-inventor of the color photography process, Leopold Godowsky Jr. Mannes admired the show's score and was inspired to arrange a meeting between Wilder and a New York theatrical producer, Dwight Wiman. Wilder later recalled:

> So I took Frank Baker along, a friend who had sung most of the songs in the show and knew them all. The appointment having been set, we rode down on the Empire State Express the day before. Standing on the open observation platform on a lovely June evening he sang me "Stormy Weather." I'll never forget the effect it had on me. God bless Harold Arlen!
>
> The next morning we presented ourselves at Mr. Wiman's office to be told that Mr. Wiman had gone unexpectedly to the Middle West. So we turned around and came back to Rochester. Much later we found out that Mr. Wiman's assistant had planned to listen to us, but obviously the news had not reached the receptionist.
>
> Okay, ask me! Why didn't we go back? Why weren't new appointments made through Leopold Mannes's good offices? I haven't the faintest notion, nor have I ever been able to figure out any reasonable explanation. I don't think I'm a masochist and, although I did have enough money at that time, I can't believe I wouldn't have been happy to get a little acceptance. (*Life Story,* 47–48)

Wilder imagined that if he had persevered, "it might have turned me into a show writer, successful, probably" (*The Search*, 68). But this, he wrote, is a "ghastly speculation." In any case, he was not destined for a singular career; he would never be just a show writer or songwriter, or just a composer of chamber music and art songs.

Back in New York

His mostly self-designed and self-administered basic musical education behind him, Wilder shifted his home base back to New York City shortly after the *Haywire* experience in 1933. His reasons for moving were partly financial: he had spent the last of his inheritance and needed to do something to generate income.[15] But also, he surely felt that Eastman and Rochester had no more to teach him, that the next phase in his musical education had to take place downstate. Many of his Eastman friends had already made the same migration, or were headed that way. In any case, for Wilder, the move to New York involved no major planning or strategizing. He lived out of a suitcase, and he simply took up permanent residence at the Algonquin Hotel on West Forty-fourth Street, where his family had always stayed when they visited during his childhood. (He later confessed that he had even stayed there when visiting the city during his Eastman years, unbeknownst to his mother, residing farther uptown.) The hotel staff knew him well and accommodated his eccentricities, and of course he always had the freedom to disappear into a passenger train on the spur of the moment. For the rest of his life, despite extended stays with friends from time to time, and extensive travels, he would consider the Algonquin his only real home.

Starting in the mid-1930s, Wilder essentially lost focus on the varieties of concert music that had so impassioned him back in Rochester. Instead he devoted more and more attention to pop songwriting, as he had since parting company with Eddie Brandt around 1930. Surviving (unpublished) song scores from these years, with music and lyrics by Wilder, have titles such as "Incurably Romantic," "Once in a Million Years," and "Why So Much Talk about Love?"[16] His lyrics in these songs are simple and direct and consistent with current songwriting practices. "Just One" is typical:

A Just One
Under the sun
Gives me such devotion
Just as deep as the ocean
No wonder, I am in love.

A Just One
Under the sun
To my heart keeps bringing
Love that makes it keep singing
Just One.

B You are my beacon of light
One star out of the night
We'll walk into the dawn
Just you and I.

A Just One
Under the sun
Or in stormy weather
We'll be always together
Just One.

The song's musical form is likewise standard, with symmetrical four- and eight-bar phrases fitting snugly within thirty-two-bar AABA conventions. The other songs in the collection also follow these popular norms, although some have prefatory verses that may be slightly less formulaic.

Whether writing in the popular style or setting existing poetry for concert songs, at this point in his life Wilder thrived on regularity of form. His work shows an interest in working within established structural norms, not in modifying or redefining them. It was "marvelously exciting" to set poems by James Stephens, he wrote, "partly because the form is created for me by the poems themselves" (*Letters I Never Mailed*, 88). At the same time, he was becoming more and more aware of the differences between art-song setting and pop songwriting. An existing poem has its own style, its own drama, its own music. If it is good, it stands on its own and does not require musical interpretation (or lighting, or dramatic staging) to enhance its impact. A popular-song lyric, however, is written to be sung and cannot exist independently; it needs music to make it complete. In Stephen Sondheim's words, music "liberates a lyric."[17] Whereas an art-song writer must work hard to respect the poetry, taking care not to undermine or contradict its inherent power, a pop songwriter works back and forth between two mutually dependent dimensions, coaxing them to nurture and complement each other. Indeed, in a successful popular song the sense of "dimensions" falls away entirely, leaving only the thing itself, the artful commingling of text and music.

Wilder's willingness to follow convention in the forms of his early songs left him free for adventure in other arenas, particularly harmony. Even songs based on fairly routine progressions (e.g., "It's All Done with Mirrors," "Lovely") are often enlivened by moments of chromatic interest. Many feature greater extents of chromatic movement throughout (e.g., "Sunlight's Got Me in Between," "You Incredibly Lovely Human Being"). Others are harmonically fresh and imaginative in other ways, with surprising twists or unusual individual sonorities (e.g., "Why So Much Talk about Love?"). These songs show that Wilder had been absorbing influences astutely, not only when listening to Jerome Kern or George Gershwin on the Victrola or at the theater but also while getting to know music by Wagner and Debussy back at Eastman. In this respect, these songs are not commonplace at all and seem intent on challenging conventions and finding a distinctive voice. As Wilder put it, "I couldn't turn out the ordinary song. My sights were too high, and I couldn't, no matter how hard I tried, write straightforward, unsophisticated tunes" (*Life Story*, 61). It is easy to believe his account of a publisher's reaction after Wilder showed him some of these early efforts: "We can't sell any of that Juilliard shit" (*Letters I Never Mailed*, 105).

Wilder is undoubtedly referring to a song like "Once in a Million Years." This song's bridge, for example, features one of his less singable melodies, at first unfolding notes of a diminished triad (G on "it only," B♭ on "one single," C♯ on "Never it"), later widening its intervallic range to fourths and fifths (Example 2). The harmonic support winds evasively around D major but includes half- and fully diminished seventh chords and an augmented sixth sonority at the final cadence (the "French" type, until the melody moves up to A♯ on "of"). The music is more than simply an expressive representation of a broken heart; the sounds in this

Example 2: "Once in a Million Years," bridge

song were typical of Wilder's harmonic palette throughout this and many other works of this time period.

Some of the early songs did eventually gain wider exposure. "Time and Tide" was originally part of a revue, *Thumbs Up!* when the show began a pre-Broadway tryout in Philadelphia in November 1934.[18] It is harmonically lush like the other early pop songs, with a catchy tune and standard AABA structuring, preceded by a verse infused with chromatic lines. To a sophisticated listener it might have sounded right at home next to other songs in *Thumb's Up!* such as Vernon Duke's "Autumn in New York." The show's primary decision makers found the song expendable, however, and by the time the show premiered in New York in December, "Time and Tide" had been dropped.[19] Other Wilder songs from this period emerged on the radio a few years later. "Give Me Time" was first recorded by Mildred Bailey in 1940 and later by other artists, including Johnnie Ray (1951) and Jeri Southern (1952).[20] Helen Forrest sang "Soft as Spring" with the Benny Goodman Band in 1941.[21] "Trouble Is a Man" was eventually recorded by Sarah Vaughan (1948), Judy Holliday (1958), and Ella Fitzgerald (1969), among others.[22]

Wilder's inscription at the top of his score for "Time and Tide" reads, "Words and music by Alexander Wilder." At some point soon after he wrote that song, however, he began to change his signature. He explained, "For popular music I'm shortening my name to 'Alec' as Alexander looks so pompous" (*Letters I Never*

Mailed, 102). It was also during this time that he began working as a commercial composer-arranger for New York studios to generate income: "I was forced to write a lot of music under extremely unpleasant circumstances as well as orchestrate many songs I despised" (*The Search,* 78). His Eastman friend Jimmy Caruana, who had also changed his name, to Jimmy Carroll, and who was already emerging as a prominent commercial arranger, helped him get work and showed him the ropes. They worked together on arrangements for a band Carroll wanted to start (*Life Story,* 68). According to Wilder, Carroll "taught me almost everything I know about arranging" (*The Search,* 90).

What exactly did he teach him? Wilder had already written for orchestra a few years earlier at Eastman, after all, and he surely had a basic familiarity with the instruments. But a popular-song arrangement is its own art form. Differences in style and instrumentation aside, the pop arranger is much more of a creator, more of a collaborator with the originator of the tune and text. Wilder explains: "Arranging, after all, is a euphemism, for it includes composition as well as orchestration. The introductions, countermelodies, transitions, reharmonizing are all more than just orchestration. But by using the word 'arrangement' they get two skills for the price of one" (*Letters I Never Mailed,* 102). A pop arranger's primary mission is to preserve a song's melody and lyric. Everything else is open to creative manipulation. The arranger has substantive control over the way the song is presented and received, even over elements such as chord changes that were likely integral to the songwriter's original conception. Wilder called it an "unwritten rule": "Arrangers may alter the harmony of the sheet music to suit themselves."[23]

He occasionally got himself in hot water for exercising too much creative control in dance-band arrangements. He remembers scoring "Sleepy Time Down South" (Clarence Muse, Leon T. Rene, Otis J. Rene Jr. [1931]) for Mildred Bailey to sing with the Benny Goodman Band and including an "unexpected harmony" intended to "make it a little less obvious and cliché[d]" (*Letters I Never Mailed,* 106–7). Goodman disapproved, forcefully and publicly.[24] While working on the arranging staff of *The Ford Hour* on CBS radio in 1936, Wilder similarly revised Cole Porter's harmonies in "It's De-Lovely" (from *Red, Hot, and Blue!* [1936]). Wilder recalled, "Even the Bach-oriented organist-conductor could sense the ineptness of my alterations and spoke rather harshly to me from the podium" (*Life Story,* 72).

In his arranging projects, Wilder also joined a current trend toward recasting classic concert literature in jazz style. The idea had been around for a while, at least since Paul Whiteman's "Song of India" (1921), a swing arrangement of an aria from Rimsky-Korsakov's opera *Sadko* (1897), but had lately gathered steam in recordings such as Raymond Scott's "Minuet in Jazz" (1937), which was a restyling (including a conversion from triple to duple meter) of Paderewski's Minuet in G (from *Humoresques de concert*, op. 14, no. 1 [1886–87]), and Alec Templeton's "Bach Goes to Town," a pastiche of baroque clichés arranged by Henry Brant and recorded by the Benny Goodman Band in 1938.[25] The trend especially flourished in 1939, in swing versions by the Raymond Scott Quintette of the first movement of Mozart's C major piano sonata, K. 545 ("In an Eighteenth-Century Drawing Room") and of the quartet from Verdi's *Rigoletto* ("A Little Bit of Rigoletto"); and in swing versions by the John Kirby Sextet of Chopin's C♯ minor Fantaisie-Impromptu ("Impromptu") and Dvorak's "Humoresque." Wilder remembers making swing arrangements of Bach's Little G Minor Fugue (which "kept every note but had everyone play dance style"), Ravel's "Pavane pour une infante defunte," Debussy's "Golliwogg's Cake-Walk," and Kreisler's "Tambourine Chinois" for the CBS radio show (*The Search*, 90; *Life Story*, 72; *Letters I Never Mailed*, 103). These efforts only enhanced his reputation for oddity and iconoclasm; they drew a "flood of perplexed letters" and "made the players very happy but elicited black frowns from the men handling the advertising account" (*Letters I Never Mailed*, 103).

Wilder's initiation was now complete. Since making the decision to focus on music in his late teens, in the mid-1920s, he had schooled himself in the banjo and piano and musical notation, and Eastman had given him a basic foundation in the craft of concert-music composition and orchestration. When he was in his twenties, he had also started to develop as a writer of popular songs, first in partnership with Eddie Brandt, and then on his own. Now, in the years surrounding his thirtieth birthday in 1937, he had been through basic training in the art of arranging and orchestrating for the popular market. He was finally ready to progress beyond reliance on the work of others, either for primary inspiration or for actual material, and follow a course that was more unique and personal.

2 Breakthroughs

First Professional Successes in the 1930s and 1940s

IN THE LATE 1930S, with the United States moving from economic depression to global military conflict, the Swing Era was reaching its zenith in the recordings and radio broadcasts of big bands led by Duke Ellington, Count Basie, Benny Goodman, Artie Shaw, Tommy Dorsey, and Glenn Miller. Smaller groups like the John Kirby Sextet and the Raymond Scott Quintette flourished as well, playing original compositions or arrangements of popular songs by Irving Berlin and George Gershwin and other pillars of American songwriting. Alec Wilder remembered the flavor of the center of the jazz world, West Fifty-second Street in New York, during that time and into the next decade: "Fifty-second Street was in full cry about that time, 1939. I came to know it much better than I would have normally because of Mabel Mercer and Cy Walter. . . . Every great jazz instrumentalist and singer was to be found there during those years, from Art Tatum to [later] Marian McPartland, from Billie Holliday to Sarah Vaughan, from Dizzy Gillespie to Max Kaminsky" (*Life Story*, 72–73). Wilder was a frequent patron of the street's many jazz clubs, after days spent peddling songs to publishers or writing arrangements for radio programs. It was not exactly the life that he had earlier imagined for himself, but the sounds he was absorbing, on top of the variety of other musical experiences he had had up to that time, would serve him well for the next phase of his career and beyond.

The Alec Wilder Octet

Alec Wilder's first big impact on the music of his time, a series of short pieces with unusual instrumentation that he wrote between 1938 and 1940, came about through the support and persistence of his Eastman friend Mitchell Miller. In the 1930s, Miller was one of the premiere oboists in New York. Virgil Thomson called him "one of the two or three great ones at that time in the world."[1] Miller played oboe in the Mannes Concerts at the Metropolitan Museum of Art, in orchestras led by Fritz Reiner and Andre Kostelanetz, and in the pit orchestra for the first run of *Porgy and Bess* (1935). He claimed to have declined an offer to be appointed principal oboist with the New York Philharmonic because it would have entailed a pay cut.[2] As a studio musician with the CBS Symphony, he had been in the orchestra for Orson Welles's infamous *War of the Worlds* broadcast in 1938. He was also a loyal and supportive friend who had helped Wilder get work as a dance-band arranger with CBS. Wilder called him a "roaring dynamo" whose "energy and enthusiasm comprise an irresistible force" and who "used to come to the Algonquin to encourage and prod me" ("The Tuxedo," 31–32; *Elegant Refuge*, 72–73).

The story of Wilder's emergence into the public arena begins with a professional association between Miller and the harpsichordist Yella Pessl in the mid-1930s. Their names appear together in several notices about musical events in the *New York Times* during this period, including a lecture-recital for the American Woman's Association (April 20, 1936) and concerts of Baroque music at Town Hall (March 20, 1938, and January 20, 1939) and at the David Mannes Music School (April 17, 1938). Pessl had told Miller about a film project she had taken on that called for a swing version of a classic harpsichord piece, in the spirit of recent recordings by Raymond Scott and Benny Goodman, and Miller had put her in touch with Wilder. Wilder recalls, "I had found a Couperin piece for harpsichord that suggested jazz rhythms, but before I put an arrangement on paper I asked Miss Pessl for permission to familiarize myself with her harpsichord. She allowed me to visit her apartment, and in the course of experimenting with her German-built instrument I fell in love with the sounds it produced" (*Elegant Refuge*, 73). Pessl's film project never reached fruition, but Wilder would remain fascinated with the harpsichord and on the lookout for opportunities to use it in the years to come.

Perhaps he had also begun to think differently about the harpsichord after speaking with his friend John Barrows, who had written pieces for the instrument that were performed by Ralph Kirkpatrick at the Yaddo Festival in Saratoga Springs in September 1938.[3] Barrows might have told him about another piece on the same program, Robert McBride's "Harpsipatrick Serenade," that took the harpsichord out of the seventeenth century and into the twentieth, with swinging rhythms and richly stacked modern harmonies.

In any event, the harpsichord was very much on Wilder's mind when he kept an appointment that Miller had made for him to demonstrate some of his songs for an influential executive at Brunswick Records, probably sometime in 1938:

> The night before the appointment I stayed out very late and drank far too much. I hadn't been asleep three hours when the phone rang. Mitchell shouted me awake. I'll never know how I got myself shaved and dressed. I was as hung over as I had ever been in my life.
>
> By the time I got to the recording company's audition room I was scarcely able to sit upright on the stool. What I sang, let alone played, I shall never know. But I do distinctly recall that poor Joe Higgins, the Brunswick official, was in a state of bewilderment. Mitchell was muttering and fidgeting, and little wonder. For I had messed up whatever good fortune might have resulted from the audition.
>
> However, Joe Higgins, a kindly and gentle man, was too polite to send me packing, so after making some bland remarks about the songs I'd sung, he asked me if I wrote instrumental music. I admitted that I did, and that I was interested in becoming a serious composer.
>
> He then asked me if I could write some pieces in the manner of Raymond Scott, who had recently written and recorded a number of successful instrumentals for Brunswick Records, all with odd, even incongruous, titles such as "Dinner Music for a Pack of Hungry Cannibals." Hung over as I was, my head splitting, my lips parched, I managed somehow to speak convincingly of my ability to write as well as Scott.
>
> When asked what instruments I would use, naturally I thought first of the oboe, Mitchell's instrument. Then I added flute, bassoon, clarinet, bass clarinet—all woodwinds—and, suddenly, I recalled the marvelous sounds the harpsichord made. So I added that. Later I added bass and drums for rhythm. Thus, haphazardly, I arrived at an octet.[4]

Wilder then wrote one short piece for that instrumentation, and Miller brought together some of his colleagues with the CBS Orchestra to meet at Yella Pessl's apartment for a reading. A representative of Brunswick, Morty Palitz, was on hand and liked what he heard. So Palitz scheduled a recording date for a woodwind quintet of Mitchell Miller (oboe and English horn), Jimmy Carroll (clarinet), Eddy Powell (flute, doubling on clarinet), Harold Goltzer (bassoon), and Toots Mondello (bass clarinet), along with the harpsichordist Walter Gross and a rhythm section of Frank Carroll (bass) and Gary Gus (drums).[5] Wilder wrote three more pieces for the same instrumentation, and all four were recorded on December 19, 1938. He would go on to write fifteen more octets for five additional sessions held between March 1939 and August 1940 (see "Selected Works," section II). On the labels of the records that were ultimately released, in 1939 and 1940 on Brunswick and Columbia, the group was identified as the Alec Wilder Octet.

The titles for the pieces were pure silliness, usually indicating nothing, or very little of substance, about the music so named. The title for the first one, "A Debutante's Diary," is simply autobiographical, not musically evocative. Wilder said that some of the titles were "inside jokes" with friends: "The Children Met the Train," with the songwriter-arranger Kay Thompson; "It's Silk—Feel It," with Eastman friend Sam Richlin.[6] The titles range from pedestrian ("Please Do Not Disturb") to playful ("Bull Fiddle in a China Shop") to cryptic ("Dance Man Buys a Farm"). They seem to draw inspiration from recent recordings by the Raymond Scott Quintette, including the one Wilder mentions, "Dinner Music for a Pack of Hungry Cannibals," and also "Twilight in Turkey," "Reckless Night on Board an Ocean Liner," and "The Girl with the Light Blue Hair" (all released in 1937). Scott's predecessors in fanciful titling included Reginald Foresythe ("Serenade for a Wealthy Widow" [1933]; "The Autocrat before Breakfast" [1934]) and Red Norvo ("Dance of the Octopus" [1933]). More recently, John Kirby had made a similarly conceived record titled "Rehearsin' for a Nervous Breakdown" (1938). Perhaps Wilder was also inspired by some of Erik Satie's titles, such as "Trois morceaux en forme de poire" (Three pieces in the form of a pear [1911]) or "Véritables préludes flasques (pour un chien)" (Genuine flabby preludes (for a dog) [1912]).

Wilder's later collaborator James Maher told Desmond Stone that the titles and the musical ideas in the recordings by Foresythe and Norvo (less so Scott) influenced Wilder's conception of the octets.[7] All were part of a trend in the 1930s toward an unconventional conception of jazz, rejecting tune-based improvisation in favor of the composed piece, the fully notated artwork. As Gunther Schuller has noted, "Jazz in the form of miniature compositions, especially with catchy nonsense titles, was very much in the air in 1938."[8] Wilder also surely knew music of the recent past by classical composers that borrowed and adapted elements of jazz. Indeed, he had already made a jazzed-up version of an early example of ragtime borrowings, Debussy's "Golliwogg's Cakewalk" (from *Children's Corner* [1908]). He had probably also heard, or at least knew about, Stravinsky's appropriations of ragtime idioms in *Ragtime for Eleven Instruments* (1917–18) or *Histoire du soldat* (1918). Closer to Wilder's octet conception was Milhaud's *La création du monde* (1923), an orchestral score (ballet) replete with jazz-inspired syncopations and melodic inflections. Then there was the tradition of "symphonic jazz," in music commissioned and performed by the Paul Whiteman Band in the 1920s—Gershwin's *Rhapsody in Blue* (1924), George Antheil's *Jazz Symphony* (1925), and Ferde Grofé's *Metropolis* (1928), among others.[9]

Wilder's advantage was that he could approach the hybridization from either direction. As an experienced dance-band arranger, he could use a pop-style conception as a starting point and introduce elements of concert music, perhaps an elegant soaring melody or a rhythm that stays on the beat. He could also work easily from classical models, evading stylistic purity with jazz-inflected melodic figures or harmonic twists. And he was just as comfortable resting right in the center of the interplay, refusing to allow either side to dominate the discourse. The result could be described as a hybrid or composite style, but it mostly defies characterization and is simply *sui generis.*

Instrumentation plays a major role in the formulation. The clarinets and flute can easily move back and forth between jazz and classical styles, simply in the way the instruments are played. Their tone colors alone do not identify them with one tradition or another. The oboe and bassoon, however, stubbornly resist jazz adaptation. Wilder called this the "tough problem of the unswinging double reed" (*Letters I Never Mailed,* 116). In his octets, whenever at least one of these instruments is playing, the aura of the concert hall has an unmistakable presence. Virtually everything else happening in the score could be drawn from jazz traditions, from the swinging rhythms to the harmonic language, but if the sound of the oboe or bassoon is prominent, the overall effect cannot come across as pure jazz. What makes many of the octets interesting are the ways Wilder handles this issue, which can range from embracing the inevitability to masking its effect to placing the double-reed sound in an ironic frame.

The harpsichord can be surprisingly versatile. We are culturally conditioned to associate its sound with old concert or chamber music, but a stylish performer can easily overturn such preconceptions. Artists discovered this in the years following the first Wilder octet recordings, in records by the harpsichordist Sylvia Marlowe (*Bach to Boogie Woogie* [1940]) and by Johnny Guarnieri playing harpsichord with Artie Shaw and the Gramercy Five (e.g., "Special Delivery Stomp" [1940]).[10] Wilder felt that the harpsichord in his octets was a "most colorful and properly percussive background for attemptedly swinging legit woodwinds" (*Letters I Never Mailed,* 116). He often used it as a mediator between the mellower flute and clarinets and the more assertive, stylistically typecast double reeds.

Wilder's sensitivity to and handling of all these issues are already apparent in the first octets he wrote, the four that were recorded on December 19, 1938. The second piece on the session, "Concerning Etchings," has roots on the jazz side of the continuum, featuring a swung refrain played in octaves (Example 3a) and close jazz harmonies mimicking a big-band saxophone section (Example 3b).[11] A plaintive tune appears in straight rhythms in the oboe (Example 3c), as if trying to pull the style to the other side, followed by a similar effort in the bassoon, but

Example 3: Excerpts from "Concerning Etchings" (pencil short score, TRO Archive)
a. "refrain"
b. *tutti* harmonic treatment
c. main melody

the swinging single reeds refuse to let it happen. Later, when the clarinet and flute play the same tune, it sounds completely at home in jazz style.

By contrast, the next piece on the December 19 session, "A Little Girl Grows Up," approaches the interplay from the other direction. Most of its gestures and rhythms sound more at home in a concert hall, starting with a series of stately chords in the harpsichord (Example 4a). This leads to a lyrical melody in the English horn and other passages with only occasional hints of popular idioms. Eventually, a swinging Benny Goodman–style melody in the clarinet seems to want to bring the piece over to the other side (Example 4b). It never does, although it never stops trying.

Example 4: Excerpts from "A Little Girl Grows Up"
a. harpsichord, mm. 1–6
b. clarinet (concert pitch), mm. 17–20

Page 1 of Wilder's pencil score for "A Little Girl Grows Up." (*TRO Archive*)

The final recording on that first session, "Neurotic Goldfish," embodies yet another approach to the stylistic interplay. Here the musical ideas seem more distinct from each other, set up more to contrast than to merge. The music moves back and forth between sounds leaning toward jazz and gestures familiar from concert music, using instrumentation to help make the affiliations. An often-heard series of triplet figures sounds like it belongs in a concert work for orchestra or small chamber ensemble. When it appears around the midpoint, it accumulates a *Petrushka*-like diatonic saturation (Example 5a). In contrast with the triplet passages, a series of big-band-style chords appears in syncopated rhythms (Example 5b). At one point, the two elements play off each other in rapid give-and-take (Example 5c). The piece is a relatively rare case of a meaningful title for one of the octets, as the music seems neurotically torn between styles, in frenetic, fidgety rhythms.

The stylistic conception is most interesting, and different still, in the first piece on the session and the first one Wilder wrote, "A Debutante's Diary." Rather than evoking one style or the other, either staying close to one while hinting at another or moving back and forth between them, "A Debutante's Diary" stays right in some central zone, where everything seems fresh and new. The melodies, harmonies, and rhythms seem to belong to concert music and jazz in roughly equal measures. A soaring oboe melody (Example 6a) pulls toward the classical side, but it is perfectly balanced by its bouncy, jazzy accompaniment (Example 6b). When all the instruments play together, we think of a big band, but the tones of the double reeds and harpsichord are just incompatible enough to defy easy categorization. Given the task of writing a piece for popular distribution, to be recorded by this combination of instruments, it would have been easy for Wilder simply to write a dance-band arrangement with an unusual instrumentation. Instead he created something utterly unique, an entirely new sound. He threw out precedents and explored his imagination.

The four pieces on that first session nicely encapsulate the basic features of Wilder's stylistic amalgamations, in subsequent octets and in his work in general. On a continuum from pure concert music on one end to pure jazz on another, "Concerning Etchings" and "A Little Girl Grows Up" are firmly rooted on opposite sides of the midpoint (with crossover elements playing secondary roles), "Neurotic Goldfish" jumps back and forth from one side to another, and "A Debutante's Diary" simply roams the center. If the first two can be described as *rooted*, the third is more of a *dialogue*, and the fourth a *hybrid*. Manifestations of these paradigms appear throughout Wilder's music. A harmonic progression, for example, can be rooted in the style of concert music or jazz, with an occasional chord or chord sequence

a.

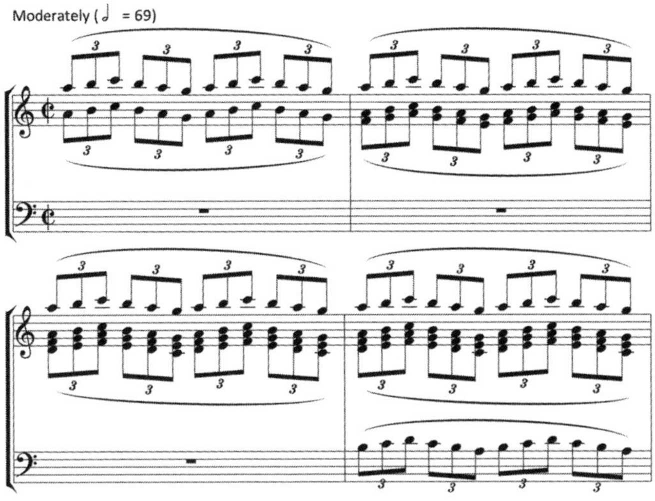

b.

c.

Example 5: Excerpts from "Neurotic Goldfish"
a. harpsichord, clarinets, bass clarinet, mm. 73–76
b. mm. 24–28 (condensed score)
c. wind instruments, mm. 45–48

Example 6: "A Debutante's Diary," mm. 39–42
a. oboe melody
b. harpsichord, drum set, bass

thrown in that evokes the other side; or it can move back and forth in dialogue, between chord patterns associated with one tradition and those sounding purely like the other; or it can be a hybrid, combining sonorities and gestures from both traditions in roughly equal (or consistently unpredictable) proportions. Rhythms can be mostly straight or mostly swung, with occasional hints of the opposite side; they can alternate between purely straight and purely swung; or they can combine the traditions in unique and inventive ways. And so forth. The strongest sense of melding comes when musical parameters evoke different traditions at the same time, as in "A Debutante's Diary." Any conceivable combination is possible and expected—hybrid harmonies in rooted rhythms, or a melodic dialogue presented by stylistically rooted instruments, and so forth. Wilder's music can sometimes seem to be anywhere on and all over the continuum at the same time.

As he went on to write and record fifteen more octets in 1939 and 1940, Wilder explored all of these possibilities and began to develop preferences and tendencies. Three of the next five, recorded in March and June of 1939, are rooted in jazz: "Walking Home in Spring," "It's Silk, Feel It," and "She'll Be Seven in May." "Such a Tender Night" is more of a dialogue. "Sea Fugue Mama" is the strongest example of a hybrid from this group, with a jazzy tune presented in the very formal manner of a fugue. Wilder explains that the tune itself, and the piece's title, were inspired by a recording by the Andrews Sisters, "Hold Tight, Hold Tight" (1939), and its catchy refrain, which begins with the phrase, "Want some seafood—mama" (*Letters I Never Mailed,* 116). In "Sea Fugue Mama," Wilder takes the central motive from "Hold Tight" and works it into a fugue subject that is presented in a fairly routine exposition and then brought back in the manner of fugal episodes. It calls to mind Milhaud's jazz fugue from *La création du monde* (1923), which helps tell the story of gods of creation emerging from a chaotic mass. Even more it is reminiscent of Benny Goodman's recording of Alec Templeton and Henry Brant's "Bach Goes to Town" (1938), which also starts like a fugal exposition, using a very similar main melody, and has a similar overall character.

In the last ten octets from this period, recorded between December 1939 and August 1940, Wilder crystallized his style and methods. If the pieces in the earlier sessions offered opportunities for working out particular compositional issues or challenges, now the matters seem largely settled. All ten are essentially hybrids, resting comfortably in the center of the stylistic continuum. Classically tailored melodies soar above jumpy, syncopated rhythms. Chord voicings and progressions borrowed from dance-band arrangements change character depending on their instrumentations. The writing for harpsichord often leaps out of the texture with particular panache, moving effortlessly among and around stylistic traditions. With these works, Wilder had truly found his compositional voice and fashioned a sound that was personal and unmistakable.

The recordings of the Alec Wilder Octet attracted a fair amount of attention starting in 1939, even if listeners were unsure what to make of them. A review of the initial release ("A Debutante's Diary" backed with "Neurotic Goldfish") in *Gramophone* magazine probably typified general reactions: "How far Alec Wilder has failed by trying to do something different for the sake of it, and how far he has scored by cooking up a form of jazz chamber music in a classical saucepan, is a debatable point, but there's plenty of food for thought in both records."[12] Wilder came to believe that he had fallen into some nebulous purgatory between musical factions: "When the [octet] records came out, they were gunned down by the jazz boys because they had a classical flavor and they were gunned down by the classical boys because they had a jazz flavor."[13] In the words of the *Gramophone* reviewer,

> Already I see the rotten eggs and tomatoes hurtling across the footlights.
>
> The biggest are coming from the swing fans. That's not surprising. Whenever jazz tries to extend its scope they make a rush for the flag of conservatism. In a way I don't blame them. Once bitten twice shy. But there's no need to carry the flag to the extreme that leads only to that rather quaint sect which refuses to consider anything new until it has become old.
>
> Equally unsavoury are likely to be the tokens from the classicists. They are certain to sneer at Mr. Wilder's efforts as just another pretentious endeavour to elevate jazz above its station.

A few years later, an article in *Downbeat* summarized the reactions from one side, in a column titled "Lounging with the Longhairs": "That's the trouble with [Wilder's] music—it reeks peace and pasture at every bar. It's all very fine for a while, but you wish along about the fifth tune that someone would come in with a real off-tune, tailgate New Orleans trombone, and break things up. The music gets too precious, lusher than any sweet band ever thought of being."[14]

As time wore on, however, the octets gradually gained acceptance and appreciation from all directions. Wilder recalled receiving accolades from Dave Brubeck and Igor Stravinsky (*Life Story*, 57). In 1941, the composer-author Sigmund Spaeth called the octets "delicious stuff that everyone will enjoy" and announced Wilder's achievement with an effusive proclamation: "For people who have good taste in music, but are likely to be a little bored by the conventional classics, I have a surprise this year. America has produced a new composer of real individuality. Some of us have known about him for quite a while, but all of a sudden the discerning public is catching on. His name is Alec Wilder, and he has written some of the most charming and original music since Gershwin—which is high praise."[15] Wilder's activities within musical circles in New York began to be tracked in magazines and newspapers.[16] Finally his years of study and on-the-job training in practice rooms and radio studios were beginning to pay off. He claimed not to have welcomed the attention, but that was part of the bargain.

At least the notoriety helped him get new work—not just menial labor but more interesting projects in which he had ample creative control. During the June and December 1939 octet sessions, the same group also recorded Wilder's instrumental arrangements of popular songs: "Japanese Sandman" (music by Richard Whiting, lyrics by Ray Egan), "Blue Room" (Rodgers and Hart, from *The Girl Friend*), and "Sweet Sue, Just You" (Victor Young, Will J. Harris), for release on Brunswick and Columbia. Again the octet instrumentation gives the arrangements freshness and quirkiness. In the "Blue Room" recording, for example, the hand of the arranger is particularly conspicuous; the arrangement is almost a variation of, or fantasy on, the original song. Wilder also made arrangements for a similar group—the same octet, except with piano instead of harpsichord—accompanying Maxine Sullivan on four songs recorded in August 1939: "Turtle Dove" (Lou Singer, Bob Bilder), "Ill Wind" (Harold Arlen, Ted Koehler, from *Cotton Club Parade*), "Jackie Boy" (words and music by Lou Singer), and "Sing Something Simple" (words and music by Herman Hupfeld).[17] These arrangements are a little more straightforward but still have the capacity to surprise with offbeat instrumental colors.

Perhaps the happiest consequence of Wilder's emergence into public consciousness were the greater opportunities to meet and collaborate with some of the musicians whose work he admired. He had had the voice of Mildred Bailey (along with Bing Crosby and Ethel Waters) in his ear when he wrote some of his first popular songs years earlier. After he met Bailey and her husband, the bandleader Red Norvo, in 1938 or 1939, they became close friends and began looking for projects together. Their first was a series of eight songs that Wilder arranged for Bailey and an instrumental group consisting of woodwinds (but no bassoon), trumpet, and rhythm section, including guitar and again with piano, not harpsichord. The repertoire included popular songs, theater songs, and spirituals:

"Don't Dally with the Devil (Too Long)" (words and music by Willard Robeson)
"Sometimes I Feel Like a Motherless Child" (traditional)
"I've Gone off the Deep End" (Ralph Rainger, Leo Robin)
"I Shoulda Stood in Bed" (Ralph Rainger, Leo Robin)
"All the Things You Are" (Jerome Kern, Oscar Hammerstein II, from *Very Warm for May*)
"Blue Rain" (Jimmy Van Heusen, Johnny Mercer)
"Nobody Knows the Trouble I've Seen" (traditional)
"Hold On" (words and music by Hall Johnson)

These arrangements were recorded in September 1939 and released soon after by Columbia (some on the Vocalion label).[18] In these renditions, Wilder generally does not push boundaries or draw attention to the arranger's craft as he had in other recent arrangements (especially "Blue Room"). He is respectful and diligent, offering just enough support for Bailey's masterful vocals to be interesting, but not so much as to get in the way. As an arranger and as a composer, he had found his stride.

Back to the Stage

Wilder's earlier flirtations with Broadway, his songs for *Three's a Crowd* (1930) and *Thumb's Up!* (1934), were just the beginning of a lifelong interest in writing music for the stage. It was an abiding passion that had begun in his youth: "Even in the early years after my family had moved to Park Avenue in New York City, I spent all my vacations from nightmarish boarding schools attending every Broadway show I could scrape up the money for. Movies never attracted me as they did others of my age. No, I had to see footlights, live actors" (*Elegant Refuge*, 18). In the late 1930s and early 1940s, when he was not otherwise involved with octets and arrangements-for-hire, he pursued theatrical projects on several fronts.

One was a show called *Swingin' the Dream*, which was a jazzed-up version of Shakespeare's *A Midsummer Night's Dream*, in the spirit of other recent modern adaptations, such as Rodgers and Hart's *The Boys from Syracuse* (opened November

Wilder in his thirties. An inscription on the back of the photograph reads, "Alec Wilder in love again—1940, St. Regis." (*Alec Wilder Archive, Sibley Music Library, Eastman School of Music*)

23, 1938; based on Shakespeare's *The Comedy of Errors*) and *The Hot Mikado* (opened March 23, 1939; swing arrangements of Gilbert and Sullivan's songs by Charles L. Cooke).[19] Wilder claimed to have "written an entire score" for *Swingin' the Dream* but then "had to take it back due to the duplicitous character of the producer" (*American Popular Song*, 444). When the show opened on Broadway on November 29, 1939, Wilder was credited with just one song, "Love's a Riddle," perhaps based on a poem by the eighteenth-century playwright-poet Henry Carey. (No score survives.) The show was a bit of an extravaganza, with a cast of 150, including Louis Armstrong as Bottom, Maxine Sullivan as Titania, Butterfly McQueen as Puck, and Moms Mabley as Quince; a full orchestra in the pit plus small jazz bands on the sides (one of which was the Benny Goodman Sextet); and dances staged by Agnes de Mille. It received mixed reviews and closed after thirteen performances.

A second theatrical project during this time inaugurated one of Wilder's most enduring and important songwriting partnerships. It began in the spring of 1939 with a call from an agent who wanted to show him a script for a musical revue, including complete song lyrics, by a writer who was looking for a composer-partner. The script followed the lives of a man and woman who had known each other as children and who eventually fall in love, marry, and divorce.[20]

Wilder recalled: "I went to the agency, picked up the script, read it, and was immediately captivated by it. I called the agency and asked to meet the author. It was arranged, and I met William Engvick, a very bright, very nervous and engaging young man. I took him to a record store and played one of my woodwind octets for him. Then he, too, was captivated" (*Life Story*, 78–79). Over a weekend while visiting his friend Frank Baker's parents' house in Pennsylvania, Wilder wrote music for all the lyrics in Engvick's script. A short while later, during a visit to Connecticut, he completed music for two ballet sequences that Engvick had envisioned. Thus began a collaborative relationship and friendship that would endure for decades.

The team's debut, however, was inauspicious. The show they had written, known as *Ladies and Gents*, never got off the ground, despite persistent promoting and reworking. They arranged a read-through for some potential supporters (notably the comedy team of Olsen and Johnson) but were unable to generate interest for a "sophisticated and tender piece of work" (*Life Story*, 81). A blurb in the *New York Times* on July 22 announced that the script was available through the William Morris agency, suggesting that "it could fill the requirements of a Bob Hope or an Imogene Coca," but this too led nowhere. Three years later (on June 28, 1942) the *Times* announced that a different show by Engvick and Wilder, called *Sweet Danger*, was destined for Broadway, with the backing of Carroll Case, the son of the owner of the Algonquin Hotel. The article summarized the show's storyline: "It has to do with the pulchritudinous subject of the models of the Powers agency, but it also flashes back to the Gay Nineties, and there is a slight thread of mystery running throughout." This effort also fizzled, however, and the show would evolve through three more titles—*Brace Yourself, Brother*; *Chance of a Ghost*; *Don't Look Now*—and other potential backers and ultimate dead ends in the coming years before it was abandoned altogether, its numerous songs cast to the wind for other shows and other purposes.

Wilder was able to extract the music for the two ballet sequences from *Ladies and Gents*, known as "Life Goes On" and "The Green Couch," and place them alongside a third, new composition as separate movements of an orchestral work, *Three Ballets in Search of a Dancer*, which premiered in New Orleans in 1946.[21] Demsey and Prather indicate that the new movement, "False Dawn," was eventually retitled *Piece for Orchestra* and premiered in Rochester in November 1947, with Erich Leinsdorf conducting the Rochester Philharmonic.[22] But the *Piece for Orchestra*, as listed on the program for that concert, was actually three movements, named "Moderato," "Adagio cantabile," and "Allegro vigoroso"; perhaps the entirety of *Three Ballets in Search of a Dancer* became the *Piece for Orchestra*.

In any case, the experience may have helped Wilder think differently about his music and his ability, after reading program notes written by the Eastman musicologist Charles Warren Fox. Wilder recalls: "In his notes [Fox] revealed that there was more than the suggestion of order and discipline in my piece. He had found indications that I was better organized than I had any notion I was" (*Life Story*, 106). All the same, Wilder wrote, the score was "far from great, perhaps no more than a fair student piece."

A few years earlier, in 1941, Wilder had written music for an actual ballet troupe, on a commission from the American Ballet Theater. *Juke Box*, choreographed by William Dollar, to a libretto by Lincoln Kirstein and with scenes and costumes by Tom Lee, brought together themes from the octets to tell a story set in a college hangout (*New York Times*, May 18, 1941). The ballet was performed by the American Ballet Theater in South America in the summer of that year and by a Rochester group the following May, with Howard Hanson conducting.[23]

Song Standards

Broadway disappointments notwithstanding, the early 1940s marked the beginning of Wilder's most successful period of popular songwriting. His collaboration with William Engvick enriched and inspired him, yielding songs that have been widely performed and recorded. He also continued to write his own lyrics on occasion, and these efforts too demonstrate new levels of competence and originality. He would go on to write popular songs for the rest of his life, eventually totaling more than two hundred, but in quality and impact he would never surpass those he wrote just after the octets, when he was first emerging to prominence in the field of popular music.

In addition to the songs they wrote together during this time for their ill-fated revue, Wilder and Engvick wrote standalone songs to present to publishers (see "Selected Works," section III). "We wrote some lovely songs, only a few of which got sold, but which we had a ball writing," Wilder remembered (*Life Story*, 81). Others were just "little warming foolishnesses for occasions" ("The Tuxedo," 43). He also wrote music in a less commercial mode, in the manner of the art song, for some of Engvick's poems, with titles like "Definition," "I Liked Him Not at All," "In the Morning," and "The Shiftless Man" (all 1942). At some point Engvick created lyrics for the main themes of two of the earlier octets, "Such a Tender Night" and "Walking Home in Spring" (originally recorded on March 31, 1939). The duo's most enduring creation from the first three years of their partnership, the classic "Who Can I Turn To?" was suggested to them by Mildred

Bailey. Wilder defends the grammatical liberty in the title phrase: "My contention was that this was an instance of justifiable wrong grammar, since 'who' evoked the same lost feeling as 'where' or 'when,' 'why' or 'how.' 'Whom,' on the other hand, sounded heavy and straight from the Senate" ("The Tuxedo," 44). He has a point: in one of the first recordings of this song by the Gene Krupa Band (1941), the vocalist Howard Dulany actually changed each "who" to "whom," marring an otherwise fine rendition.[24] Fortunately, he was the only one; other recordings of this song, by the likes of Jo Stafford with the Tommy Dorsey Orchestra (1941), Lee Wiley (1956), Morgana King (1964), and Barbara Lea (1978), are gleefully ungrammatical.[25]

"Who Can I Turn To?" is a natural successor to the pop songs from the Rochester period, with strict formal regularity and sumptuous harmonies, but Wilder's melodic line now has an elegance and refinement that the earlier songs did not have. Engvick's lyric is also a vast improvement:

A Who can I turn to,
Where can I go,
How can I face it alone now,
After the moments we've known,
Who can I turn to now?

A Who can I sing to,
How can I smile,
How can I wish on a star, how?
Knowing the way that you are,
Who can I turn to now?

B We walked in the spell of the summer,
We kissed in the wind and the rain.
But now the enchantment is over,
The echo and I remain.

A People are strangers
Who walk through the town,
Ghosts in a lonely parade, oh,
Where are the dreams that we made?
Who can I turn to now?

The theme of questioning, expressing the helplessness and despair of the jilted lover, pervades the A strains, with "who," "where," and "how" questions in the first A, "who" and "how" in the second, and "who" and "where" in the last. The B strain offers a brief reminiscence of better days—and a relief from the questioning—supported in classic manner by a tonal shift away from the home key, before reality returns and "the echo and I remain." Poetic images of stark loneliness, shattered dreams, and lifeless wandering help drive home the main sentiment. Wilder's setting is an ideal expression of these ideas, as if both music and lyric had sprung from the same source—the true test of a great song.

Engvick also wrote lyrics for three songs composed by Wilder in collaboration with Morty Palitz, the record producer who had played such an important role in the recording and distribution of the octets. "Moon and Sand" has often been covered by instrumentalists (e.g., Kenny Burrell, Ellis Larkins, Keith Jarrett), and "J. P. Dooley III" was a "very happy little trifle," says Wilder (*Life Story*, 57).[26] The trio's most distinguished effort was "While We're Young," which began with a melodic phrase that Engvick had in his ear as he wrote a different lyric, "Everywhere I Look" (1945). Palitz wrote out the new tune completely as Wilder supplied the supporting harmony, and then Engvick created the new lyric.[27] Wilder was fond of quoting an Algonquin acquaintance, the writer James Thurber, saying that the lyric to "While We're Young" was "the finest piece of English writing he knew" (*Songs Were Made to Sing*, 6). Indeed, it is a model of economy and elegance:

verse We must fulfill
This golden time
When hearts awake
So shyly,
Softly.

A Songs were made to sing
While we're young.
Ev'ry day is spring
While we're young.

B None can refuse,
Time flies so fast,
Too dear to lose
And too sweet to last.

A Though it may be just
For today,
Share our love we must,
While we may.

C So blue the skies,
All sweet surprise,
Shines before our eyes
While we're young.

The lyric is perfectly nuanced and yet disarmingly simple; only five of the refrain's sixty words are longer than one syllable. Palitz's melody too is the essence of simplicity—a perfect counterpart—and Wilder seems to have restrained himself somewhat to stay clear of overly complex chord structures in his harmonization. The writers have also noted that the song was originally written in duple meter but changed to triple to enhance its commercial viability. It was quite successful, in recordings by Fred Waring and His Pennsylvanians (1946), Tony Bennett (1951), Peggy Lee (1951), Perry Como (1952), and many others.[28]

And once again a song's overall structure is absolutely conventional—not another AABA, but now the other standard option, ABAC, with uniform phrase lengths. Songs Wilder wrote on his own during this period likewise adhere to established formal models, leaving room for explorations in other areas. He remembers showing "Out on a Limb" to Harry Goodman (Benny's brother), "the only publisher at that time who would publish my tunes" (*Life Story*, 63). An arrangement of this tune was recorded by Chick Bullock and His Levee Loungers (Vocalion 5171) and used as a theme for a radio program in 1939. Wilder's AABA lyric for this song is rougher, earthier, than Engvick's elegant creations, but it does show ample growth since his efforts of ten years earlier, when he was based in Rochester:

A To tell you the truth, I'm wasting my youth
Waiting for you to decide what to do
Make your mind up, sink or swim
Or you'll be left out on a limb.

A I'm getting bored with being ignored
I'll take the cue but it must come from you
Make your mind up, sink or swim
Or you'll be left out on a limb.

B Though you're the cutest thing 'round the town
Your indecision's really bringing me down
If you intend to be more than a friend to me
Cut out your foolin' around.

A Nothin's taboo when I'm around you
You're mighty smart, but you can't break my heart.
Make your mind up, sink or swim
Or you'll be left out on a limb.

The hook (the last two lines of each A strain) is crippled by a mixed metaphor, but the lyric is otherwise charming in several ways. The rhyming pattern pairs words within phrases at the beginnings of the A strains (truth/youth, you/do in the first A), then shifts to rhymes at the ends of phrases in the hook (swim/limb). The bridge is different still (including an imprecise rhyme on town/down/around), highlighted by an unexpected return to the earlier internal rhyming pattern in the third line ("If you intend to be more than a friend to me").

Wilder's tune for "Out on a Limb" demonstrates how thoroughly he had mastered the pop idiom. The rhymes within phrases likewise have parallel or similar melodic shapes; the melody rhymes along with the lyric. The phrase at the beginning of the hook rises to the song's highest note with the imperative ("Make your mind up, sink or swim") and then falls back with the completion of the ultimatum ("Or you'll be left out on a limb"). Meanwhile, as in the past, the harmony is anything but routine and yet not a distraction or highbrow pretense. A mostly chromatic descending line, stylishly harmonized, underlies the entirety of the A sections, starting in an inner part and concluding in the bass at the end of the hook. Contrast in the bridge comes from unexpected bluesy inflections, evoking a vivid image of the "cutest thing 'round the town."

This sort of chromatic descent was a fascination for Wilder during this time, perhaps inspired by the Gershwins' "Someone to Watch Over Me" (from *Oh, Kay!* [1926]) or Rodgers and Hart's "My Funny Valentine" (from *Babes in Arms* [1937]). Wilder's classic solo effort from 1941, "It's So Peaceful in the Country," features chromaticism as well, within the main strains of another AABA form. Wilder remembers writing this song for Mildred Bailey because she was stuck in the city, "unable to get up to her country place, . . . a kind of vicarious weekend out of town" (*Songs Were Made to Sing*, 95). His lyric is conversational and descriptive, hardly poetic at all, like capturing bits of dialogue between friends who happen to rhyme a lot. That is its secret: because it is ordinary, it is peaceful. The best recordings of the song, by Mildred Bailey (1941), Tony Bennett (1959), or Meredith d'Ambrosio (1986), for instance, are likewise spare and unassuming.[29]

Wilder published his best-known song, "I'll Be Around," the following year, 1942. He had jotted down the title in a taxi in Baltimore and wrote the tune a few days later; "the lyric took much longer to write."[30] Later he was unable to recall why he wrote the lyric himself: "I'm again foggy as to why I had written my own lyrics to songs which had achieved a little notoriety, 'It's So Peaceful in the Country' and 'I'll Be Around.' I know that Bill Engvick went home to Oakland during the forties but I can't remember if he had gone when I wrote those songs. I must assume so as I would never have risked my own lyrics if he had been available" (*Life Story*, 82). "I'll Be Around" is Wilder at his most elemental—basic, honest emotions expressed with an economy of words:

A I'll be around
No matter how
You treat me now
I'll be around
From now on.

A Your latest love
Can never last,
And when it's past,
I'll be around
When he's gone.

B Good-bye again,
And if you find a love like mine,
Just now and then
Drop a line to say you're feeling fine,

A And when things go wrong,
Perhaps you'll see
You're meant for me,
So I'll be around
When he's gone.

Much of its strength comes from the interplay between music and text: the similar settings of the recurring title phrase, the rising stepwise motives highlighting rhyming couplets (e.g., "No matter how / You treat me now"), the musical pairings of rhyming phrases in the bridge. Harmonically, the song takes the idea of the scale descent from "Out on a Limb" and "It's So Peaceful" and turns it in the opposite direction, into a rising bass line, first diatonic (from step 1 up to 5 of a major scale), then chromatic (from step 5 up to 8). The sweep of the bass line and resulting chord progression have the air of something more sophisticated, more learned than typical pop harmony, as if trying to pull the listener away from a nightclub and into a concert hall.

Unfortunately, these elements are mostly missing in one of the first recordings of the song, the version that became definitive in the ears of many listeners, by the Mills Brothers (Decca-18318 [1942]). Wilder remembered his reaction to that recording in a conversation with Thelma Carpenter on a radio program many years later:

> I heard that a record [of "I'll Be Around"] had been made, and I don't think I'd had a record at that time. I went into a record store and bought it. I took it to one of those little booths they used to have years ago, played it, and it was the *wrong tune*! That is to say, the Mills Brothers

> are notorious for not listening to the guitar player, who reads music. He played the tune, but they couldn't get it. So they played the wrong—the wrong tune. I took the record back to the man—I'd already paid for it—and I said, "Just so nobody else can have this," and I snapped the record. You know, it was one of those kinds you can break. I snapped it across my knees and handed him the pieces and walked out. About sixteen records followed that, all wrong melody—including your friend George Shearing. Because he'd heard the original record. Also Johnny Smith, the guitar player—I don't know how many people. Nobody bothered to check the music. Then Mr. Sinatra, bless his heart, came along and corrected it. Of course, Mabel had sung it, Mabel Mercer had sung it, and always sang it right, but she wasn't recording then.[31]

The Mills Brothers do sing two wrong notes in the melody of their recording (on both syllables of the word "around" in the hook), but Wilder also could not have been pleased with the harmony in their arrangement, which completely abandons the song's elegant chord progression, as if sanitizing it for the popular market. Wilder could be certain that Sinatra's version got the two melody notes right because he did the arrangement himself, for release on V-disc in 1943 (Columbia 124-A). Sinatra also sang those two notes correctly—while taking customary liberties elsewhere in the tune—when he recorded a second version of the song in 1955, for his album *In the Wee Small Hours* (Capitol W-581), to an arrangement by Nelson Riddle.[32] Just as important, both arrangements feature Wilder's original harmonies. Wilder referred to Sinatra's rendition (presumably the widely known 1955 recording) as the "definitive version" of the song. Surely this does not mean that he was in any way disappointed with many other excellent versions that have appeared over the years, by artists such as Mildred Bailey (1950), Rosemary Clooney (1951), Anita Ellis (1953), and Tony Bennett (1964).[33]

With songs like "I'll Be Around" and one he wrote the following year for Peggy Lee, "Is It Always Like This?" Wilder began to emerge as a distinguished presence in American popular songwriting of the 1940s.[34] He was not temperamentally suited for the limelight, however, and often declined opportunities to enhance his visibility and professional standing. Like the man himself, Wilder's songs were much more comfortable in a dark bar than in a spotlit theater. Rather than writing a song for a publisher, with an eye toward selling records and sheet music, he preferred writing for individuals, for specific voices and sensibilities. It is an approach to songwriting that he had always taken, since his first efforts years earlier, when he had written hypothetically for Ethel Waters or Bing Crosby. Now the idols he was writing for were also his friends—Mildred Bailey, Peggy Lee, Dick Haymes, Mabel Mercer—and he could generally assume that they would sing anything he wrote for them. To hear one of his creations in the voice of a particular singer was no longer an act of imagination.

Likewise, his lyrics are intimate and personal. They speak directly from the heart, often in plain language, unadorned by colorful words or poetic images. His songwriting partner William Engvick was more poetic but cared equally about the virtues of simplicity. Their lyrics console and comfort, empathize and pity. They ask questions: Who can I turn to? Is it always like this? They value escape or dwell on abandonment. Wilder wrote his share of love songs, but he was as willing to address other topics as he was eager to avoid romantic commitment in real life. After hearing some of his songs, publishers had been known to react with questions like, "Where's the broad?"[35] Further, the art of songwriting was perfectly suited to his nomadic, rootless lifestyle, offering fleeting opportunities and neverending inspirations, one more opportunity for capturing a moment or emotion in thirty-two bars. As he moved on to other pursuits in the mid-1940s, and for the rest of his life, he would always come back to it.

Ranging Outward

As the 1940s progressed, Wilder solidified his standing in popular music with new arranging projects and original songs. He continued to explore stylistic boundaries in a new series of octet recordings. And he revived his theatrical ambitions in scores for three musicals with new collaborators. Although he was not consistently self-supporting, often depending on the generosity of James Sibley Watson, the work kept him engaged and fulfilled.[36] In a letter to Watson in 1947, he even displayed uncharacteristic self-satisfaction: "My status in the music world has become of such a nature as to baffle not only me but numbers of others (not friends). . . . Not, by the way, that I am superior, but I am good."[37]

He began an association with one of his most loyal friends and supporters in 1943, during a prolonged labor dispute between the musicians' union and record companies. The current sensation Frank Sinatra had initially been inclined to suspend recording until the strike was over, in support of the union and to get off on the right foot for his first recording under a new contract with Columbia Records.[38] As the strike wore on, however, more and more artists had been crossing the picket line, and two young rivals, Dick Haymes and Perry Como, had recently worked around the conflict by making records with all-vocal accompaniments. When Sinatra decided to follow suit, he asked Wilder to do some of the arrangements. Presumably he knew the octet recordings and the arrangements Wilder had done for one of Sinatra's (and Wilder's) favorite singers, Mildred Bailey. Wilder suspected that he was chosen for the job because of the "ridiculously small fee" he charged, "a hundred dollars apiece" (*Life Story*, 180).

Wilder has been credited for arranging three of the nine a cappella recordings Sinatra made between June and November of 1943.[39] Two were numbers from the groundbreaking Broadway show that had opened in March, Rodgers and Hammerstein's *Oklahoma!*—"Oh What a Beautiful Morning" and "People Will Say We're In Love"—and the third, "Sunday, Monday, or Always" (Jimmy Van Heusen, Johnny Burke), was a recent hit for Bing Crosby, from the film *Dixie*, in which he was currently starring opposite Dorothy Lamour. Wilder's arrangements mostly treat the voices as instruments, translating what would be sustained notes in the strings in a conventional orchestral arrangement into "ooh"s and "ahh"s. Voices sing actual words at places in the arrangement where the backing voices would typically take over the lead, such as when repeating the bridge after the soloist's initial run through the complete lyric. In general, the arrangements are competent, respectful to both song and singer, giving the sense that Wilder was on his best behavior in this opportunity to work with an industry luminary. Wilder remembers making one small change in a single chord in one of the songs from *Oklahoma!* "to make it more suitable for voices"; Richard Rodgers, listening from the booth, insisted that the original harmony be restored (*Life Story*, 182).

Wilder and Sinatra became good friends and mutual supporters. Some time after the a cappella recordings and after the musicians' strike was settled, the singer asked Wilder to make orchestral arrangements for two songs by Willard Robeson, "Old School Teacher" and "Think Well of Me." When Robeson failed to provide sheet music for the latter, Sinatra gladly allowed Wilder to substitute one of his own songs, "Just an Old Stone House"; it was released as a B-side a few years later.[40] Sinatra and Wilder's biggest and boldest project together came about in October 1944, when Sinatra was in the midst of one of his infamous concert runs at the Paramount Theater in New York. Wilder recalls: "Frank Sinatra, whom I knew quite well by then, was having an enormous success at the Paramount Theater, so great, in fact, that he was forced to stay in his dressing room except for the time that he was on stage. His bobbysoxers' intoxication over him had brought out the mounted police and it wasn't safe for him to show himself in the street. To help him while away his time, I sent over what they then called an 'air check' (a record) of the performance by Mitchell Miller" (*Life Story*, 83–84). Wilder is referring here to his *Slow Dance*, a short piece for the original octet instruments (including harpsichord) plus strings that he had written for a wartime exchange program between the United States and England. Sinatra was said to have played the record repeatedly in his dressing room at the Paramount and came to feel that Wilder should write more music of this sort. Wilder remembers: "He became so enthusiastic about it that he phoned to ask if I had any more pieces like it. Oddly, I had started writing a series of pieces for solo woodwinds and strings. He told me that he wanted to conduct them on recordings. When I managed to catch my breath I reminded him that he didn't know how to read music. He, never one to let a little thing like that stop him once he had made up his mind, said he would figure out a way to do it."[41]

Eventually Wilder completed four pieces, called "Airs," to feature soloists playing oboe, English horn, flute, and bassoon, accompanied by a conventional string orchestra, without harpsichord or rhythm section. These four Airs, along with the *Slow Dance* and one other new work for octet and strings, *Theme and Variations*, were recorded by musicians from the CBS orchestra with Sinatra at the podium in late 1945.[42] He mostly stood before them and waved his arms and cued; the group had already been rehearsed by Miller and/or Wilder. In Wilder's memory, Sinatra was able to earn the support of the musicians when he "threw himself on their mercy."[43]

Slow Dance and *Theme and Variations* are natural heirs to the octets. *Slow Dance* is mostly rooted in a classic orchestral sound with a meditative melody very much like Ravel's "Pavane pour une infante defunte" (which Wilder had earlier arranged for dance band). Contrasting passages of dance-band writing enter occasionally as if in dialogue, and in the middle there are moments of hybrid, but the overall character is rooted in the concert hall. *Theme and Variations* begins as a dialogue between a classically conceived fugue subject (Example 7a) passed around as if trying to develop a full-fledged fugue, contrasting with music that seems to belong in a dance hall (Example 7b), with the fugal materials dominating the discussion. As the piece progresses, however, the styles come closer together and eventually merge: the previously stodgy theme gets support from jazzy chords and rhythms, while the dance-hall style becomes absorbed into a hybrid sound.

If the stylistic elements of these two pieces are engaged in some sort of battle or contest, the dynamic gives musical voice to an inner conflict that Wilder may have been experiencing as well. Having spent so many recent years devoting most of his energies to popular styles, he now found himself being pulled back toward the sorts of concert music that he had first explored more than a decade earlier. Indeed, the four Airs on the Sinatra record have almost no elements of jazz or popular music—ironically, perhaps, because the stylistic blending of the octets and *Slow Dance* are presumably what inspired Sinatra to make the record in the first place. In excellent performances by the soloists Mitch Miller (oboe and English horn), Julius Baker (flute), and Harold Goltzer (bassoon), themes in the Airs weave and soar above lush, tonally mobile harmonies, with clear debts to Debussy and Poulenc. While the pieces are unfailingly "pretty," however, they are formally rather aimless. They leave the impression that they are part of some context that the listening experience alone leaves incomplete, like hearing

Example 7: Excerpts from *Theme and Variations* a. beginning of fugue subject (viola and cello, mm. 1–6) b. wind instruments, mm. 143–48

a soundtrack without seeing the film. One wonders whether an experienced conductor could have shaped them more convincingly.

Wilder's renewed interest in concert music also brought him back to his calling card, the octet genre, for recordings in July 1947 and a release in September, using the same instrumentation, and mostly the same performers, as he did for the previous set.[44] The new titles follow the playful trend of the earlier ones:

"Jack, This Is My Husband"
"They Needed No Words"
"The Amorous Poltergeist"
"Little White Samba"
"Remember Me to Youth"
"Footnote to a Summer Love"

Taking part in the whimsy are the album's (anonymously written) liner notes, such as: "'The Amorous Poltergeist' describes the mood of a playful ghost—an 'innocuous phantasm'—who haunts in a 'harmless, flippant fashion'—and who, having fallen in love, feels the futility of his ectoplasmic state, and the realization that his love can never be consummated." Wilder is not in exploratory mode in these octets but is content to work within the creative framework he had earlier established. Two of them, "They Needed No Words" and "Footnote to a Summer Love," are rooted on the jazz side of the continuum, with only hints or spurts of concert-music style. These two are in fact very similar to each other, not only in conception but in many musical details, as if one is a variation on the other. The other four fit the definition of hybrid exactly as Wilder had already worked it out, blending ideas from different traditions to create something new. In "Jack, This Is My Husband," for example, a melody in swing eighths is supported by a series of jazz-inflected chords based on a half-step descent (Example 8). But the melody itself, apart from its rhythmic presentation, is a fairly square presentation of gradually widening intervals, unfolding a rising chromatic line to mirror the chromatic descent in the bass, and the harmonies themselves have just enough unusual dissonances to inhibit connotations of pure jazz. These octets represented a good project for Wilder at that time, a way to elevate his work above the ordinary, to remind himself of the value of making something more interesting than a stock arrangement of a pop song.

His return to theatrical songwriting in the late 1940s may have fulfilled a similar purpose. It began, modestly, with two children's records, both involving orchestras conducted by Mitch Miller. In *Herman Ermine in Rabbit Town* (1946), John Garfield narrates Malcolm Child's story about friendship and racial prejudice over constant background music and with three Wilder songs interspersed.[45] In *The Churkendoose* (1947), Ray Bolger recites a story by Ben Ross Berenberg about acceptance, with a score by Wilder that includes background music, interludes, and one song (Decca CU-103). From these minidramas Wilder moved on to larger musical-theater projects, including ten songs for a show called *Star of Texas* (1947) and six for a show he worked on with Edward Eager and Alfred Drake known as *Seventy-Six* (1949). Neither was completed.

A show that did make it to the stage inaugurated Wilder's association with his second important collaborator. Arnold Sundgaard had begun to establish himself as a dramatist by that time, with original plays such as *Spirochete: A History* (1938), which was a dramatization of the war against syphilis that opened in Chicago and toured the Northeast, and short Broadway runs of his original plays *Everywhere I Roam* (1938; coauthored with Marc Connelly), *The First Crocus* (1942), and *The Great Campaign* (1947). He also cowrote (with Leonard Louis Levinson) the libretto for an operetta, *Rhapsody*, with music by Fritz Kreisler, that played briefly on Broadway in 1944. After Wilder had met Sundgaard through William Engvick, Sundgaard had proposed a musical based on a play by Charlotte Berry, *Way Up Yonder*, which was an adaptation of the biblical book of Job set in

Example 8: "Jack, This Is My Husband," mm. 89–92, oboe (melody), clarinet, bass clarinet, bassoon

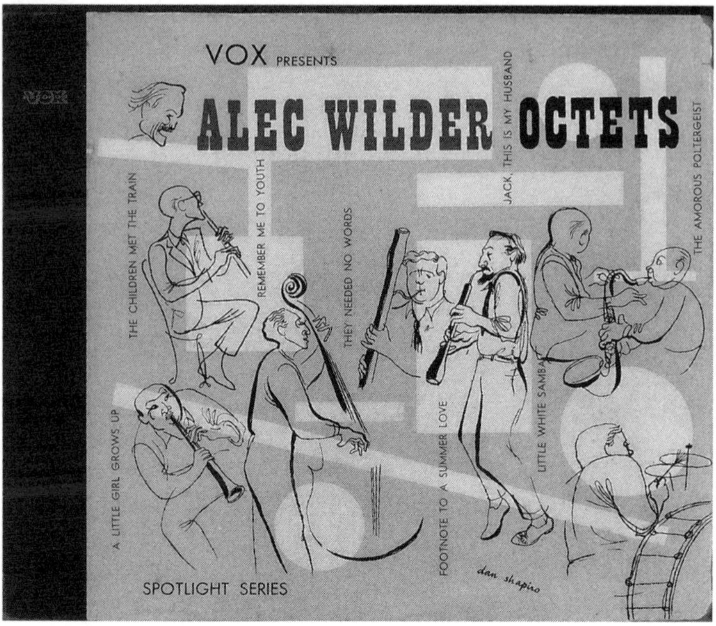

The cover of the 1947 Vox octet album (Vox 16061-16064) shows caricatures of the musicians: Eddie Powell, flute; Jimmy Carroll, clarinet; Frank Carroll, bass; Harold Goltzer, bassoon; Mitch Miller, oboe/English horn; Dick Wolff, harpsichord; Reggie Merrill, bass clarinet; and Gary Gillis, drums. Wilder looks on from upper left. In addition to the six new works, the collection also includes new recordings of two pieces from the original octet sessions several years earlier ("A Little Girl Grows Up," "The Children Met the Train").

the Colorado mountains. Wilder and Sundgaard worked on this project, which they first called *The Wind Blows Free*, starting in 1948 and saw the work staged in August 1950 at a summer festival not far from the city.[46] They revised it under a new title, *Western Star*, in 1975 for workshop performances by college students in Connecticut.[47]

The new collaborators wrote ten songs for the original version of *The Wind Blows Free*. Many of them are more intimate and artful than songs Wilder had written earlier in the decade, consistent with his general movement away from mass-market popular music during this time. Not that he had abandoned conventional formulas altogether—he did continue to write separate pop songs to fulfill professional commitments or as the spirit moved him—but he was also searching for new trails to blaze. An instrumental "Square Dance" that he wrote for *The Wind Blows Free* includes surprising changes in the meter, sudden appearances of three-beat or five-beat measures amid an overall four-beat foundation, that could give a dancer fits. Harmonies in some of the songs are unlike those usually heard in show tunes. One of the two songs that have survived outside of the show, "Douglas Mountain," is essentially a folk song, known to many children (and their parents) from a 1977 album by the popular Raffi (*More Singable Songs*, Rounder CD-8052). The other, "Where Do You Go?" appeared on Frank Sinatra's *No One Cares* album in 1959 (Capitol SW-1221). Its depressing lyric—Wilder called it a "morbid ballad about suicide"[48]—takes an unconventional form:

A Where do you go when it starts to rain?
Where will you sleep when the nighttime comes?

B What do you do when your heart's in pain?
Where will you run when the right time comes?

C These are the things that I want to know.

A Where will you hide when the lights are low?
Where do you go when it starts to rain?

D Where will you sleep when the nighttime comes?

Wilder's C phrase, the only line in the lyric that does not ask a question, breaks up a rhyming couplet with the next line, which is the return of the A material. Then the reprise of the lyric's initial couplet ("Where do you go . . . / Where will you sleep . . .") is broken up between the second phrase of the A reprise and the D phrase. This misalignment of poetic rhyme and musical phrasing builds a sense that the song, like the distressed questioner, is falling apart as it reaches its end.

When Sundgaard first approached Wilder about doing a show together, Wilder, who was staying with friends out of town, responded: "I'm through with New York. I never want to see it again. I'm not going back to New York, ever!"[49] He had had his fill of slimy producers and duplicitous publishers. He had watched his friend and supporter Mitchell Miller begin to move over to the dark side, abandoning the oboe and thinking more about popular taste and music as a product (and changing his professional name to "Mitch"). In Wilder's words, "the Bitch Goddess got him" (*The Search*, 64). But just as Wilder had ultimately accepted Sundgaard's offer, he could never stray far from the city, never give up on ambitions to be a presence in the musical culture that the metropolis embraced and embodied. What would change was the way he envisioned that presence.

3 Evolutions

Compositional Maturity in the 1950s

FROM THE LATE 1940S THROUGH THE 1950S, Alec Wilder pursued a long-held goal with growing confidence and perseverance. Having made his name as a songwriter-arranger, he now aspired to become more of a "composer." He never abandoned the popular song; in a way, the popular song abandoned him, in the voices and antics of Buddy Holly, Jerry Lee Lewis, and Elvis Presley. "As the new amateur, noisy, clumsy, tasteless writers came into power," Wilder later recalled, "it became increasingly less fun to try to write a respectable, professional, stylish, tasteful song" (*The Search*, 92). But he did continue to try, even as he found himself drawn more and more to the sounds and artistic sensibilities of the theater, opera house, and concert hall.

Wilder's turn toward concert music was also inspired, in his mind, by his association and friendship with his Eastman *confrère* John Barrows. After Eastman, Barrows had gone on to San Diego State Teachers' College and Yale, followed by a few years in the horn section of the Minneapolis Symphony in the late 1930s. During the war he was assistant leader of the Army Air Forces Band. He then settled in New York and played with the New York City Opera and New York City Ballet orchestras in the late 1940s, along with freelance work in recording sessions and radio orchestras. Eventually he would turn to teaching, at Yale, New York University, and the University of Wisconsin at Madison.[1] Wilder called Barrows "the greatest musician I have ever known" (*The Search*, 64). Barrows took on a role for Wilder's concert music that Mitch Miller had once played for Wilder's experience in the popular realm: promoting him, helping him find opportunities, and offering boundless encouragement. Wilder wrote of Barrows, "I knew that there never could be a more powerful influence in my musical life. For one thing, he believed that I was a composer. Many others believed only that I was a songwriter, but because they were fond of me, [they] smiled affably when I spoke of my other writing and offered a transparent kind of lip service. From the time he came to New York to this moment [1972], John has remained the reason I still try to write music."[2] Over the decades of their friendship, Wilder would write not only because of Barrows but also for him, as a soloist and in chamber groups. Music of this type, for small forces, usually performed in intimate settings, was a natural fit for Wilder's modest self-image and sense of his own place in the musical firmament.

Opera

Wilder's turn away from popular culture in this period led him not only to chamber music but also to opera, a genre he had not previously explored. Of course, his operatic conceptions were hardly Wagnerian in scope, more on the order of the "chamber opera" for small casts, telling simple stories. And unlike some of his other writing for voices in popular songs, Wilder always depended on a collaborator for the words he was setting and for story and character development and dramatic organization.

He may have first discussed operas and libretti and potential projects with Arnold Sundgaard during this time, but his initiation into the genre came about after had begun writing songs with a new acquaintance: "Sometime in the late forties I started working with a rather fey young man who had been begging me to write with him. Bill Engvick had gone back to Oakland where he was working in a record store for some abysmal salary. The New York commercial scene had been too much for him, the people dismayed him, and not enough good had happened for him to want to linger in an alien land" (*Life Story*, 111). The "fey young man" was Marshall Barer, then working as a commercial artist but also trying to build a résumé as a writer. Barer would find success on Broadway about ten years later working with Mary Rodgers as the lyricist and cowriter of *One upon a Mattress.* Wilder first set one of Barer's poems, "River Run," as a colorful art song in the late 1940s. They then wrote conventional pop songs for commercial releases: "I'll Dance You," a throwback to the operetta waltz, with the sounds of the oboe and bassoon standing out in the backing orchestra (recorded by Eddy Howard and His Orchestra);

"Milwaukee," arranged in the vocal style of the Andrews Sisters (recorded by Kitty Kallen and anonymous backing singers); "I'm Headin' West for a Rest," evoking the Western frontier (recorded by Dick Jurgens and His Orchestra); and "Whippa-Whippa-Woo," a bluesy number backed by a stylish big-band arrangement (Sarah Vaughan, orchestra under the direction of Norman Leyden).[3]

Although Wilder found Barer difficult to work with, the collaboration endured for several years, and they began to set their sights on something more ambitious than a three-minute pop tune: "Finally [Barer] shimmered up (he did move like a dancer) with the libretto for a full-length opera. It was called *The Impossible Forest.* He claimed that a rich friend had agreed to pay me a sum which was sizable for those days if I would compose the music for it. This I did, and then Rogers Brackett, a brilliant friend and maverick radio director, decided that he wanted to produce it" (*Elegant Refuge*, 70). In a letter postmarked January 5, 1950, Wilder wrote James Sibley Watson that Jerome Robbins ("one of the three most demanded and talented choreographers in New York") had heard the music and expressed interest in doing staging and dances for the work.[4] Eventually, however, Hanya Holm, the choreographer for a current Broadway hit, *Kiss Me, Kate,* committed to designing dances for the production (*New York Times*, January 20, 1950). Lemuel Ayers, the legendary scene designer whose credits included the original productions of *Oklahoma!* and *Kiss Me, Kate* (for which he won a Tony), agreed to do the set and costume design. Wilder wrote Watson that the opera was "slanted for children" but had "ample perverse entertainment for adults." In the *Times* (January 20, 1950) it was described as a "musical fairy tale."

After the score of *The Impossible Forest* was complete, Wilder had a recording made of the orchestra part for certain sections. Then, in a series of weekly get-togethers in the Stratford Suite of the Algonquin Hotel in late 1949 and early 1950, singers performed excerpts, accompanied by the orchestral recording, for potential financial backers and theatrical cognoscenti. Wilder recalled,

> Before we knew it, these Sunday evenings had become a fashionable event to attend. All manner of prominent theatrical and literary people came. I recall that one Sunday evening Leonard Bernstein and Marc Blitzstein volunteered to help us get the right balance between the orchestra recording and the "live" voice of the leading singer. I don't think Nancy Walker missed one of those Sunday evenings. Once we held the "curtain" for the arrival of Mary Martin. . . . One evening I happened to look up from my hot seat at the piano to see William Faulkner and Ruth Ford sitting in the first row of chairs.[5]

Despite all the attention, they were never able to raise the eighty thousand dollars needed to stage the work on Broadway. Wilder later found out that Barer himself, not a "rich friend," had provided funding for the initial work and auditions.[6] Even so, Wilder may have been able to see it on stage two years later, in a production announced by the *Times* (October 28, 1952) for the holiday season, and again in 1958 at a dinner theater in Westport, Connecticut.[7] He may not have known about a 1962 production of the opera by the After Dinner Opera Company; when he fortuitously discovered that that company was planning a production of the work in 1967, he threatened legal action and had the production terminated.[8] Among other objections, he had reason to believe that his original music had been revised or supplemented or otherwise altered without his authorization.[9]

In the immediate aftermath of the initial fizzle, Wilder was eager to explore the operatic genre further, just not with Barer. He began collaborating instead with Arnold Sundgaard, who had written a libretto for Kurt Weill's folk-themed chamber opera *Down in the Valley* (1948) prior to his first collaboration with Wilder on the musical *The Wind Blows Free* (see chapter 2). After Weill's death in 1950, Schirmer, who had published *Down in the Valley*, encouraged Sundgaard to add further to the operatic repertoire, and he began working again with Wilder. They wrote three short operas that are direct descendants of *Down in the Valley*: *The Lowland Sea* (1952), *Cumberland Fair* (1953), and *Sunday Excursion* (1953).

These four works, along with Menotti's *Amahl and the Night Visitors* (1951), Bernstein's *Trouble in Tahiti* (1952), and others, have been called "workshop operas" or "school operas." They are modestly proportioned, with small casts and minimal staging requirements, performable by schools or colleges or amateur groups. Wilder recognized that these projects "limited one's musical fancy to a degree" by narrowing vocal ranges and restraining technical vocal expectations, yet he welcomed the challenge because "they posed all sorts of useful disciplines" (*Life Story*, 114). He later recalled: "We had fun writing them, people had fun performing them, and invariably some shining talents emerged in some aspect of the production. And God knows they were grateful for them as the only alternatives were the grand operas which were impractical, or the hack operas which were sterile" (*Life Story*, 114). In other words, after an ambitious disappointment such as *The Impossible Forest*, Wilder was glad to move on to projects with greater performance prospects and wider potential appeal. In 1955 the *New York Times* reported that Wilder's three school operas plus Weill's *Down in the Valley* had been performed more than 150 times in forty-six states during the 1953–54 season.[10]

The first Wilder-Sundgaard opera, *The Lowland Sea*, borrows more than general conceptual foundations from Weill and Sundgaard's *Down in the Valley*. Both are based in folk traditions and use a familiar folk tune as a recurring theme and motivic source. Indeed, Sundgaard's description of his work with Weill could also describe his first opera with Wilder:

> Its unfolding of a tragic romance was intended to follow in extended form the shape and progression of a traditional ballad. Other equally familiar songs were introduced to heighten action and establish character. Where necessary for the plot the words were rewritten, an act of audacity justified only by the fact that the folks who sing these songs are constantly revising them themselves. The music, too, was remolded by Kurt to give it a unity of its own; the new songs were immersed in the orchestra, as it were, and permitted to rise again as arias and duets. . . . At several points in the libretto I had not been able to find traditional songs to serve the necessities of the story. It became necessary to write both words and melody that would, we hoped, blend with the rest. "Neo-folk" it might be called out of kindness; "pseudo-folk" it should be called in all honesty.[11]

In *The Lowland Sea*, the folk tune "Bobby Shaftoe" provides the starting point and inspiration for a poignant story about a sailor going away to sea and leaving his lover to wait for his return. Fragments of that tune and of others, traditional and newly composed, wash ashore throughout the score, in a harmonic language that remains generally true to the musical traditions of folk music and sea shanties.

The Wilder-Sundgaard chamber operas from 1953, *Sunday Excursion* and *Cumberland Fair*, are lighter in tone. In *Sunday Excursion*, four college students casually meet on a train from New York to New Haven and discover unexpected romantic possibilities. In *Cumberland Fair*, a girl makes dates with three different boys for a day at the fair but eventually goes home with none of them, leaving the boys glad to explore other romantic options, including the girl's cousin. Musically, the 1953 operas are also quite different from *The Lowland Sea*. *Cumberland Fair* has the feel of a classic operetta, except in moments when the harmonic language offers tastes of more complex, jazz-inspired harmonies. Like in the octets, Wilder moves comfortably between harmonic idioms, making the transitions and interactions seem organic and natural.

Sunday Excursion is the most widely performed of the three. Since its premiere by the Grass Roots Opera Company in New York in April 1953, it has often appeared on programs with other chamber operas such as Ralph Vaughan Williams's *Riders to the Sea* (at Brigham Young University in 1954), Mozart's *Der Schauspieldirektor* (at the University of Idaho in 1954), Puccini's *Il Tabarro* (at the Hartford School of Music in 1956), Douglas Moore's *Gallantry*, which also has a libretto by Sundgaard (at the Brooklyn Museum in 1960), and Menotti's *The Telephone* (at the Brooklyn Academy of Music in 1968). *Sunday Excursion* was performed at the Friends of Alec Wilder concert in New York in 2010. In this score the harmonic language is different still—more Debussy than Offenbach, often with modal flavorings and stacked thirds in parallel movement. The music is fresh and charming and inventively supportive to the dramatic structure (predictable though it may be), especially when the four main characters are musically paired and intertwined as they muse aloud about their circumstances and romantic prospects. After Harold C. Schonberg wrote an unflattering review of the piece in the *New York Times* (April 18, 1953)—he called it a "trifle," with a "construction [that] is about as subtle as an isosceles triangle"—Mitch Miller rose to its defense, noting that its "reception up to this summer of 1953 has been little less than extraordinary" and finding virtue in its "simplicity without starkness, naiveté without overtones of satire."[12]

Also belonging with the Sundgaard operas, although not commissioned or published by Schirmer, is an operatic adaptation of the Chicken Little story that Wilder made with William Engvick around the same time, with the title *Miss Chicken Little.* In a relatively rare exercise in the art of pastiche, Wilder gives each main character its own stylistic signature: the music for Chicken Little herself is often reminiscent of Rossini; Cocky Locky evokes Gershwin; Turkey Lurkey's music seems to be inspired by Gilbert and Sullivan; and the sleazy Fox sings in the style of a French cabaret song. When the characters interact, we often hear an interplay of styles as well, as when Chicken Little adds coloratura flourishes to the beguine groove of the Fox's big number, "Don't Deny." The work was premiered on November 24, 1953, in Spring Valley, New York, by local amateurs directed by Frank Baker. Shortly after that, CBS broadcast a professional production on its "Omnibus" show featuring Jo Sullivan in the title role (first aired December 27, 1953). It has been revived occasionally since then.

Wilder's five operatic excursions with Barer, Sundgaard, and Engvick in 1949–53 ultimately served as warm-up exercises for a more ambitious project with Engvick in 1955, a full-length, two-act opera first known as *The Long Way* (later *Ellen*). Engvick crafted the libretto by expanding his own short story about a thirteen-year-old girl who takes a mystical detour on a trip to the store and finds herself in an action-packed fantasy involving a gangster with the face of her father, the shooting death of an Italian film producer, and her dream lover, who turns out to be a jerk. Wilder wrote that he had "never had a more satisfying musical experience than I did working on [Engvick's] luscious libretto. I'm afraid I made him constantly nervous by writing the music so fast that I kept catching up on his writing of the libretto. I couldn't help myself, for the words begged being set to music" (*Life Story*, 138–39). Indeed, his music is comparably lush and interesting, with echoes of Puccini and Milhaud and occasional jazz infusions. By this time he clearly felt comfortable with his own musical language, with the style of his librettist, and with the art of operatic creation.

Wilder was intimately involved with the premiere of *The Long Way* at Nyack (New York) High School on June 3 and 4, 1955. He supervised the production and depleted his savings to help meet operating costs. Frank Baker, his good friend since the Eastman days, produced the show and sang multiple roles, and Rogers Brackett, who had been a producer of *The Impossible Forest*, directed. Emanuel Balaban, another Eastman friend, conducted an eleven-piece orchestra that included players from the octet recordings and other New York studio veterans. The role of the girl was played by June Ericson, who would work as an understudy for Judy Holliday in *Bells Are Ringing* on Broadway a short time later. Wilder described the finished product as "absolutely beautiful" (*Life Story*, 139).

Local critics had high praise for every facet of the production of *The Long Way*, mentioning music that was "delightful in mood and tone" (Vivian Hinternhoff, *Ramapo Valley Independent*, June 9, 1955), a libretto that was "crisp, clever, humorous, and charming" (Mariruth Campbell, *Rockland County Journal-News*, June 6, 1955), and the performances of all the singers. They noted that the show played to capacity audiences and essentially overruled a disparaging, dismissive review in the *Times* (by John Briggs, June 4, 1955). The following month, Wilder recounted the experience in a letter to his friends Jackie Cain and Roy Kral: "The audiences were enthusiastic, I spent all the money I had, and that, said John, is that. But at least I've finally seen and heard something of my own done precisely as I wanted it done—and that's worth going broke for."[13]

Songs and Shows

Wilder's collaboration with Engvick on *Miss Chicken Little* and *The Long Way* and other projects during the mid-1950s flourished in part because they were living in close proximity. Both had taken up residence in a remodeled barn near Stony Point, New York, less than an hour up the Hudson River from the city and in the same area as the homes of Mitchell and Frances Miller, John Barrows, and Frank Baker. The group of friends socialized frequently and gave Wilder a rare sense of family, while the setting itself inspired and invigorated him: "Birds and chipmunks and deer, great flowering tulip trees, brooks and hills and even general stores. . . . Breakfast at a window looking out on morning glories and an undisturbed stretch of sloping land. 'Scrabble' in the evening and maybe one more playing of *The Wee Small Hours* album of Frank Sinatra in which he sang one of my songs ['I'll Be Around']. I suppose that's what life is: work, a room with a view, laughing with friends, safe sleep, and a tacitly accepted knowledge that there is still time and probability for surprises" (*The Search*, 127).

Stony Point became Wilder's home base for the better part of ten years in the 1950s and early 1960s. He still had a room waiting for him at the Algonquin

Hotel when he wanted to stay in the city, and he was still inclined to disappear without warning into passenger trains destined for Rochester or Milwaukee or points unplanned, but when he returned to Stony Point, he was able to do some of the most productive work of his life. "It was out there at Bill's," he later wrote, "that I really, totally concentrated, with minimal interruptions, on composition" (*Life Story*, 135).

He had actually renewed his association with Engvick a short time before they moved to Stony Point, when an opportunity arose to write songs for a movie musical, *Daddy Long Legs*, a new adaptation of Jean Webster's novel about an orphan girl and her rich benefactor.[14] Engvick had been working in a record store in Oakland, California, but agreed to rendezvous with Wilder in Los Angeles, where they shared living quarters in the guest house on the estate of Douglas Fairbanks in Beverly Hills in the winter of 1952. Inexperience with Hollywood customs and personalities aside, they thrived on the seclusion and synergy and wrote songs with titles like "The Moon Just Winked at Me" and "All I Want to Do Is Dance." Wilder called it "the best score for a musical I've ever written" (*Letters I've Never Mailed*, 173). They also changed their working method: rather than using a complete lyric as a starting point, as they always had before, Wilder wrote all the melodies first (*Life Story*, 132). In the end, however, their efforts came to nothing, as the studio shelved their songs and rethought the entire project with new screenwriters and songs by Johnny Mercer, including the classic "Something's Gotta Give."[15] Only one of the rejected songs survived the experience: Mabel Mercer sang "The Family Is Home" "for a few years at the Christmas season" (*Life Story*, 134).

After they had set up shop in Stony Point, Wilder and Engvick continued producing new songs, in addition to working on *The Long Way* and other things. Some of their songs were recorded over the next several years, and some were recorded later or simply stored in Engvick's trunk (see "Selected Works," section IV). The recording label for two of their songs released by Johnnie Ray in 1952, "Don't Say Love Has Ended" and "Love Me," indicates that the orchestra was conducted by Wilder's frequent accomplice Jimmy Carroll; presumably Carroll or Wilder (or both) also did the arrangements. Marlene Dietrich's recording of "Time for Love" is a classic cabaret-style ballad, a perfect match for the star's sultry voice. Wilder and Engvick's songs from this time span a typically wide range, from 1920s dance-hall style ("Good for Nothin'"), to middle-of-the-road pop songs ("Crazy in the Heart," "A Heart to Call My Own"), to jazzy ballads ("Wish Me Well," "The April Age"), to a harmonically rich torch song ("The Lady Sings the Blues"). In "Parker's Lament" (1954), a harpsichord is a prominent backing sound, presumably a Wilder/Carroll touch. Formally, Wilder remains faithful to AABA or ABAC conventions, with rare deviations or extended or truncated phrases. Lyrically, the songs display a mastery of image and rhyme; Engvick can be clever or sentimental, direct or evocative, with equal elegance.

Wilder continued collaborating with other lyricists during the 1950s as well (see "Selected Works," section V). Some of the resulting songs were purely commercial ventures (such as "Basta," with Marshall Barer; "Low in the Lehigh Valley," with Jack Lawrence; "There's Doubt in My Mind," with Arnold Sundgaard), while some make distinguished contributions to the tradition of the American popular song ("You Weren't There," with Ruth Poll; "Love among the Young," with Norman Gimbel; "Rain, Rain" with Marshall Barer). In Wilder's pop songs of this period, we can also see the growing reemergence of loftier artistic aspirations, of qualities unusual for typical radio fare. "The Winter of My Discontent," for example, indulges the language of chromatic harmony, even while staying true to the conventions of AABA structure and regular phrasing. The lyric by Ben Ross Berenberg, taking inspiration from Shakespeare, seems to belong as much in a poetry collection as in a songbook:

A This is the winter of my discontent,
Like a dream you came and like a dream you went
Before I had a chance to know what rapture meant
Came the winter of my discontent.

A Now ev'ry trifle has become a care
Now there is no joy but only deep despair
For now your lovely vision haunts me ev'rywhere
In this winter of my discontent.

B The world is full of dissonance,
The scheme of things is wrong,
The air resounds with the resonance
Of a harsh and spiteful song.

A Now all the follies of the world seem small,
Let the empires rise and let the heroes fall
And let the ruins burn for there's no love at all
In this winter of my discontent.[16]

Wilder called it a "strange" lyric and an "angry song."[17] That it is, but it also has an infectious, haunting melody, and it has had many champions, including Jackie Cain and Roy Kral (who first recorded it in 1956), Marlene VerPlanck, Anthony Newley, Helen Merrill, and Bill Dobbins.[18]

The first page of Wilder's pencil score for "The Winter of My Discontent." (*TRO Archive*)

In songs like this, Wilder was lingering naturally and comfortably around traditional boundaries between pop songs and art songs, between entertainment for the masses and esotericism. At the same time, he was rekindling his interest in songs conceived purely within art-song traditions, possibly working his way back toward the dividing line from the other direction. Scores survive for settings of poems by established poets such as e. e. cummings ("Songs of Innocence"), Siegfried Sassoon ("Suddenly"), and Karl Jay Shapiro ("Travelogue for Exiles"), and by familiar collaborators such as Arnold Sundgaard ("I Lost My Love in Scarlet-Town"). Most of these manuscripts are not dated (or published) but are among the collection that Wilder was apparently thinking of when he recalled writing a "great many concert songs" during the years at Stony Point.[19] He may have heard but a single read-through performance of many of them, by the singer for whom he wrote them—the "best vocal musician I have ever known," Frank Baker (*Life Story*, 135). Notable exceptions were an art song he wrote to his own text a few years earlier, "Did You Ever Cross over to Sneden's?" which Mabel Mercer included in sets at jazz clubs; and two songs performed by the baritone Rand Smith at Carnegie Recital Hall on April 24, 1948, "Lost in France" (poem by Ernest Rhys) and "Gone" (Carl Sandburg).[20]

Nor had Wilder abandoned aspirations in the musical theater in the 1950s. Just after he and Arnold Sundgaard wrote their three chamber operas, they also created a light musical, *Kittiwake Island*, that premiered in 1954 at the Interlochen music camp in Michigan.[21] Sundgaard conceived the story, about scholars and their students studying a rare bird on a tropical island who eventually become more interested in studying each other. Unfortunately, the show did not enjoy the same success as the operas, and Wilder and Sundgaard reworked it a few years later for a short run off-Broadway. (Lainie Kazan had a small part.) In a *New York Times* review (October 13, 1960), Howard Taubman found little to like in Sundgaard's story, although he had good things to say about the songs "When One Deems a Lady Sweet" ("has a Gilbert and Sullivan quality"), "It's So Easy to Say" ("reminds one of [Richard] Rodgers"), "If Love's Like a Lark" ("an attractive love duet"), and "Nothing Is Working Quite Right" ("an original trio"). Indeed, the music for *Kittiwake Island* is tuneful and endearing and deserves more attention than it has received.[22]

In the latter part of the decade, Wilder continued to find time for theatrical projects of various sizes, with mixed results. He and Engvick placed two of their older songs in *Once Over Lightly* (1955), a revue starring Zero Mostel and Jack Gilford, with sketches by Mel (then known as Melvin) Brooks.[23] In 1957, Wilder and Sundgaard wrote at least twelve songs for a musical adaptation of Ibsen's *Peer*

Gynt, known as *Riley Randall*, but never saw their work on stage. A project with Barer the following year, called *Breath of Air*, suffered a similar fate, as did a set of songs for a show with Sundgaard, *Hide and Seek*, in 1960. Wilder and Engvick had better luck with a made-for-television musical version of *Pinocchio* broadcast by NBC on October 13, 1957, produced by David Susskind. Yasha Frank had originally written the adaptation, which is entirely in verse, for the Federal Theater Project in the 1930s, before the release of the Disney animated film in 1940.[24] The title role was played by Mickey Rooney, who had begun to work more and more in television dramas at that time, supported by a familiar face from Broadway and Hollywood, Walter Slezak, as Gepetto, Fran Allison (the "Fran" in the popular children's television show *Kukla, Fran, and Ollie*) as the Blue-Haired Fairy Queen, and Stubby Kaye, known for originating the role of Nicely-Nicely Johnson in *Guys and Dolls* on Broadway and on film, as the Town Crier. Wilder and Engvick's score includes a perky song about the circus ("Happy News"), a birthday song aimed directly at young viewers ("The Birthday Song"), and a stately melody Wilder had written in the forties, now reimagined as a bedtime song ("Lullaby"). The star of the score was "Listen to Your Heart," an elegant ballad conveying the story's central theme:

verse Such a confusing world, little man,
And so many things to learn,
So many choices that you have to make,
So many ways you can turn,
But if you trust your heart, little man,
And make it your guiding light,
You'll be absolutely sure to know what is right.
So when you hear its sweet secret song
Take heed and you can't go wrong.

A You will find your love somewhere, some day,
If you just listen to your heart.

A And all sweet longed-for things will come your way,
If you just listen to your heart.

B For hands can only touch, and eyes can only see,
But hearts can understand and whisper, "There's the one for me!"

A So dream, young dreamer, but be wise, be smart
And always listen to your heart.

Wilder's music skillfully complements the understated charm of Engvick's lyric. The song manages to appeal directly to the children in the target audience without pandering to them. Even so, and despite a well-received cast album released shortly after the broadcast (Columbia CL-1055), Wilder felt that his efforts were largely overlooked. "It is a fact that new songs written for television never become hits, even though the audience numbers millions," he wrote (*Life Story*, 155).

He was never able to embrace the new medium, and he claimed never to have even watched *Pinocchio* when it was broadcast: "I had no desire to look at a little television box" (*Life Story*, 154). All the same, he and Engvick signed on for a follow-up project shortly thereafter, the first television version of *Hansel and Gretel*, also written by Yasha Frank and produced by David Susskind. The show was first broadcast by NBC on April 27, 1958. Again big stars packed the cast: Hansel was played by Red Buttons, known for his earlier comedy-variety television show and for a recent Oscar-winning role in Joshua Logan's film *Sayonara* (1957); Gretel was Barbara Cook, who had just begun her Tony-winning run as Marian Paroo in *The Music Man* (opened December 19, 1957); Hans Conried, a film and television actor who had also been in the original cast for Cole Porter's *Can-Can* (1953), played the Witch; and the parents were played by Rudy Vallee, who was making the transition from popular recording artist to dramatic actor, and the opera star Risë Stevens, who was known for her portrayal of Hänsel in Engelbert Humperdinck's operatic version of the same tale (composed in 1893). Wilder and Engvick's songs followed some of the same models as their songs for *Pinocchio*, in a peppy opening number ("The Hansel and Gretel Song") and a catchy children's song ("What Are Girls Made Of?"), but they also drew from operetta traditions in "Men Run the World" (reminiscent of Sigmund Romberg's "Stout-Hearted Men"), "Market Today" (featuring dialogue between soloist and chorus), and "Evening Song" (modeled after the "Evening Prayers" duet in Humperdinck's opera). In "Eenie, Meenie, Mynie Moe," Wilder expanded his harmonic palette a bit wider, employing playful chord progressions in support of the whimsical lyric ("N-trie, mintrie, q-trie corn / Appleseed and berry thorn / Apple high and berry low / Once again, here we go . . ."). Again a cast album came out shortly after the broadcast (MGM E3690), and again Wilder was disappointed with the meager recognition he received for his efforts (*Life Story*, 156).

His focus on the ears and sensibilities of younger viewers in these two shows was part of a general trend reaching back at least as far as *Churkendoose* and *Herman Ermine* in the 1940s and encompassing a series of songs he and Marshall Barer wrote for Mitch Miller's Little Golden Records series, with titles like "The Happy Man and His Dump Truck" (1950), "Timmy Is a Big Boy Now" (1950), and "Poor Mr. Flibberty-Jib" (1951). In 1955, *Downbeat* reported that Wilder had been writing children's songs for Little Golden Records for "the last eight years."[25] His and Barer's most expansive contribution to the cause of musical appreciation for young listeners was *A Child's Introduction to the Orchestra* (1954), conceived with the same educational aims as Benjamin Britten's *Young Person's Guide* (1946) but using songs rather than narration to make the introductions. Of course, Mitch Miller conducted and demonstrated the oboe, while other friends sampled the bassoon (Harold Goltzer, who had played on the octet sessions), double bass (Frank Carroll, also an octet veteran), and French horn (John Barrows). Wilder later confessed to being a bit embarrassed by the names someone had supplied for the different instruments ("Knute the Flute," "Bobo the Oboe," "Poobah the Tuba," and so forth), but overall he was pleased with his attempt to spark musical interest in children (*Life Story*, 113). The finale is a suite of four short movements featuring all the instruments and based on a single theme, like a miniature version of what Britten did over the course of his entire work. According to the *Downbeat* article, Wilder's piece "brought forth some startling statistics as well as some of the most extravagant praise ever given to a work of this sort."

The uncredited *Downbeat* reporter also observed that Wilder's music for children represented one of four dimensions of his work, along with songwriting, composing for orchestral instruments, and writing the "urbane, slightly off-beat," ultimately unclassifiable octets. Finally, as he approached his fiftieth birthday, his public image had caught up to his private ambitions.

Underscorings

Wilder's work for stage and screen in the 1950s also included musical contributions of a very different sort, drawing not from his experience as a songwriter but from the work he had done as an orchestrator and arranger and, earlier, as an aspiring symphonist. In 1950 he wrote incidental music for Arthur Laurents's second Broadway play, *The Bird Cage*, which was not well-received and played for only twenty-one performances. A second similar assignment soon after, to add additional musical moments in support of Leonard Bernstein's songs for a version of *Peter Pan*, fared better and ran for 321 showings between April 1950 and January 1951. And in 1952, Lemuel Ayers, an accomplice on *The Impossible Forest* project, persuaded Wilder to write incidental music for N. Richard Nash's *See the Jaguar*, a famous five-performance flop because the cast included James Dean making his Broadway debut in a small role. (Wilder had briefly counseled and looked after Dean when he first moved to New York and had helped him get an audition for the part.[26]) Wilder's background music for the show was purely choral, without instrumental accompaniment, to save money.

Wilder got involved in film scoring through his friendship with Hugh Martin, the songwriter of standards such as "The Boy Next Door" and "Have Yourself a Merry Little Christmas" (both from the Vincente Minnelli/Judy Garland film *Meet Me in St. Louis* [1944]). In the late 1940s Martin had written songs for a film by Jerome Hill about the artist Grandma Moses, and Wilder had done all the arranging, not only for the film itself but also for an expanded *Grandma Moses Suite* that was recorded and released in 1950 (Columbia Masterworks LP-5634). Wilder had to do more than just orchestrate; he also had to guess "what direction the music might have taken had the composer expanded it," trying to "extend the melodic lines in [Hugh Martin's] style of writing" (*Life Story*, 143). As Martin later said, Wilder's work "transcended orchestration and became composition."[27] Martin thought of himself as "strictly Tin Pan Alley" and therefore incapable of doing more than crafting a tune, and he was elated with Wilder's expansions.[28]

Apparently the filmmaker was pleased as well, for Jerome Hill engaged Wilder a few years later to score a film about Albert Schweitzer, the author and humanitarian especially esteemed for his study of Johann Sebastian Bach (1905). Wilder did not warm to the project right away; he felt intimidated by the subject's stature in the field of music scholarship, and he had heard that Schweitzer had requested Arthur Honegger to write the score (*Life Story*, 143). But Wilder soon discovered that Hill was a generous and inspirational collaborator who made all accommodations to showcase Wilder's efforts. The composer came to sense a mystical connection with film and filmmaker: "Strange things happened. I would write a cue knowing only its subject and mood, not its length. A piano track would be made and run with the film footage. On many occasions they would end simultaneously. The final spooky coincidence occurred when a motif I had written to announce Dr. Schweitzer's first appearance on the screen and had used in occasional two-measure cadences throughout the score was present only when Schweitzer appeared on the screen. This was unplanned, unintended except for the first time" (*Life Story*, 144). Wilder later called Hill "the easiest person I had ever worked for" (*Life Story*, 144). The film won the Academy Award for Best Documentary Feature in 1957.

After the Schweitzer film was finished, Hill was eager to work with Wilder again and had planned to make a cinematic version of the Christmas story, "built on the stained glass windows of France's famed cathedrals at Chartres, Rheims, and Laon" and featuring music by Wilder (*New York Times*, January 13, 1957). Although this project failed to materialize, Wilder composed and acted for Hill a few years later in *The Sand Castle* (1961). This was a very different conception from Hill's earlier documentaries, an atmospheric reverie about a group of random beachgoers and a boy building a sand castle, shot in black-and-white for the first fifty minutes, switching to color animation in a dream sequence at the end. Wilder expanded his music for this film into a suite of orchestral movements for a recording, conducted by Samuel Baron, shortly after the film was released.[29] The album showcases Wilder the entertainer, in movements with names like "Swing Music" and "Lonely Seascape." A movement called "Ragtime Music" is one of his most effective comedies, with surprisingly shifting phrase patterns and slapstick juxtapositions of ragtime idioms. As the composer explained, he was "dredging up the worst clichés I could think of to make it funny."[30] The centerpiece of the score is "Variations," essentially a passacaglia that builds upon itself to dramatize the construction of the sand castle. In this and all the movements, Wilder seized the opportunity to exercise and cultivate his skills as an orchestrator and his long-simmering urge to compose for large ensembles.

Around that same time, he satisfied those same urges in music for a promotional film by *Life* magazine, *Since Life Began* (1961). His next film score came shortly after that, again working with Jerome Hill on a quirky story with not much plot, called *Open the Door and See All the People* (1964). This one earned even less acclaim than Hill's previous effort; in the words of one critic, "Alec Wilder's musical score, generally rollicking or poignant, is the one professional thing in the film" (Bosley Crowther, *New York Times*, April 2, 1964). But it ultimately proved to be a windfall for Wilder after William Engvick became enamored with the music and found abundant opportunities to add lyrics to Wilder's instrumental melodies. The result was six free-standing songs with lyrics by Engvick, adapted from tunes in the film: "I See It Now," "Love Is When," "Mimosa and Me," "Remember, My Child [Vespa Waltz]," "That's My Girl," and "Unbelievable." Wilder wrote his own lyrics for a seventh, "Such a Lonely Girl Am I." Because the songs were not originally written as such, many of them defy traditional phrasing patterns and formal arrangements. "Mimosa and Me," for example, is a sort of hybrid of AABA and ABAC forms. Likewise are some of the melodic lines atypical for popular songs (and not easy to sing), and the harmonies are fairly adventurous. As a group they represent some of Wilder and Engvick's most distinguished contributions to the genre, and several have become well known thanks to stylish interpretations by Frank Sinatra ("I See It Now"), Marlene VerPlanck ("Remember, My Child"), Mel Tormé ("I See It Now"), and Jackie Cain and Roy Kral (all seven).[31] These songs also represent the team's final group of collaborations; Wilder and Engvick worked mostly apart for the remaining sixteen years of Wilder's life.

Reams of Concert Music

Wilder ultimately came to regard his work in commercial music as a diversion from his primary career path, to write music for the concert hall. He also felt that he was sidetracked by an unexpected passion for gardening, at a house in rural Pennsylvania owned by the family of his friend Eddie Finckel (with whom he wrote three pop songs, notably "Where Is the One"), and by a tempestuous romance. He later reflected, "There had been a passage of nearly twenty years during which time I had kept my hand in, so to speak, but what with lack of self-confidence, pop music, earning a living by arranging, becoming obsessed with a garden and then a woman, I had never come to grips truly with what I had started out to do over twenty years before: create music more complex than a melody."[32] In a letter to the composer and good friend (and fellow Rochesterian) David Diamond dated August 1955, Wilder wrote: "I'd like to do nothing for the rest of my days but write small or large pieces for small (not large) groups. I'm really at the end of the road insofar as writing what someone else wants. I cannot adjust any more—or even at all. I must do whatever I can dig out of myself, for myself, my own way, adjusting only to the literal physical limitations of the instruments."[33] Drawing inspiration from his surroundings at Stony Point, and from the excellent musicians who were among his friends and neighbors there, he "finally got down to writing reams of 'concert' music" (*Life Story*, 124).

A tradition of informal musicales flourished on Sunday afternoons at Stony Point in the 1950s, bringing together talent from the surrounding area and musicians visiting from the city. Wilder took advantage of the compositional opportunities: "At first it was three French horns. The second Sunday it was three horns and violin. The third, three horns, violin, and bassoon. Each Sunday someone new would appear. And each Sunday there would be brand-new music for them to play. I would get the word from John [Barrows] early in the week what instruments to expect and then write and copy parts for as many pieces as I could write before Sunday afternoon" (*Life Story*, 137). From these experiences emerged a practice Wilder would follow for the rest of his life, of always writing music for specific musicians, usually good friends. It was not exactly a commission, for he did not expect remuneration—indeed, performers did not necessarily even know that he was writing for them—but it did usually offer the promise of a performance by a musician with a deep understanding of Wilder's work and artistic sensibility. The days of peddling his wares were over.

It was only natural, then, that he would begin what would become a crescendo of instrumental writing throughout the 1950s (see "Selected Works," section VI) by writing pieces for two of his closest friends, Mitch Miller and John Barrows. Miller premiered Wilder's Concerto for Oboe, String Orchestra, and Percussion at Town Hall in New York on February 15, 1950. In the composer's recollection, this was the very day that Miller began his new position at Columbia Records and so began (ironically) to retire his oboe and devote all his energies to producing.[34] Around the same time, John Barrows premiered Wilder's first Horn Concerto with the New Chamber Music Society of New York.[35] Wilder may have heard it performed again in Rochester in 1953, by soloist Peter Silverson and members of the Eastman-Rochester Symphony conducted by Howard Hanson.[36] And in 1951 Wilder wrote a four-movement *Jazz Suite* for a quartet of French horns with rhythm section (including harpsichord). Barrows and another Eastman alumnus, James Buffington, along with a young Gunther Schuller and Ray Alonge, played the horn parts for a recording of the work that same year (Columbia B-1674).

These two concertos and the *Jazz Suite* present a valuable opportunity for a progress report on the development of Wilder's compositional language at a transitional stage in his career. The *Jazz Suite* is fully rooted on the jazz side of the stylistic continuum. Only the instrumentation—the horns and the harpsichord blending with the guitar, bass, and drums—gives a sense of hybrid or crossing boundaries. Rescored for traditional dance band, the melodies, harmonies, and rhythms would sound completely at home. The lush "Serenade," for example, features an elegant, stylish melody, not like an instrumental version of a popular song but more consistent with the "concert jazz" tradition of Gershwin or Ellington (Example 9). Its harmonic support is richly seasoned with elements of jazz style.

But this was music written for a recording, for popular consumption. A concerto written for the stage of a concert hall, however, was for Wilder automatically rooted in the traditions of concert music. Much of the oboe concerto, for example, rests securely within conservative concert-music traditions. Its opening theme (Example 10) breathes the same air as melodies by Prokofiev or Milhaud or Copland. Within Wilder's work, the concerto joins a line of development from the instrumental Airs on the album conducted by Frank Sinatra (1945) and the *Piece for Orchestra* (1947); it has little in common with the hybridizations of the octets (1938–40, 1947). Only the third movement of the oboe concerto prominently features elements of jazz style, and this is mostly in the rhetoric of dialogue. Wilder's drive to focus more on concert music during this time would ultimately inspire him to spend more time exploring the classical end of the stylistic spectrum, not roaming the center.

That is what he did later in the decade, for example, in orchestral arrangements of American folk music and in music he wrote for Frank Sinatra (see "Selected

Example 9: "Serenade" from Jazz Suite for Four Horns, mm. 5–12

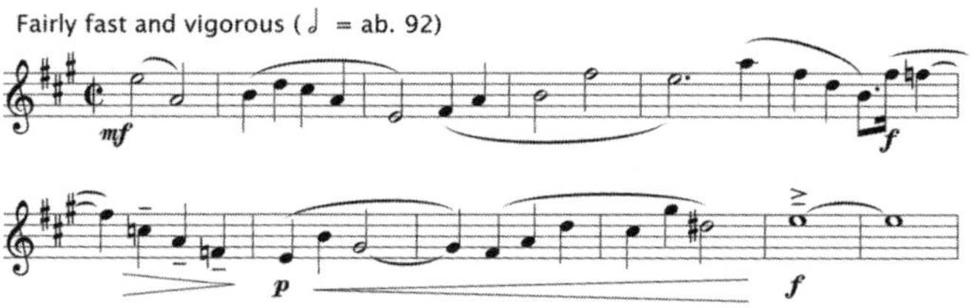

Example 10: Oboe Concerto, first movement, mm. 19–30, oboe melody

Works," section VI). The *Carl Sandburg* Suite is an utterly conventional four-movement fantasy for orchestra on tunes from Sandburg's *American Songbag* (1927), written for Carl Haverlin, the president of BMI, who was "a great Lincolniana collector, and a great friend of Sandburg's at the time."[37] Wilder received a gracious letter from Sandburg, praising the work's "quite flowing movement, never overdone," and hoping that it "moves into a permanent place on the shelf of worthy American music."[38] The music for Sinatra began with an invitation to contribute to an album of *Tone Poems of Color*, featuring music for orchestra on themes of different colors, by various popular arrangers and songwriters, and inspired by a set of poems by a writer who had worked for Sinatra, Norman Sickel.[39] The project was designed to give the singer a second opportunity to conduct, and to inaugurate the new Capitol recording studios in Los Angeles. Wilder's two contributions, *Blue the Dreamer* and *Gray the Gaunt*, are direct descendants of his earlier instrumental pieces for Sinatra (the Airs), sounding like a conservative film score and not concerned at all with breaking new ground or challenging traditional stylistic preconceptions.

And yet he was not fully committed to a single instrumental sound, during this or any other period in his life. Around the same time as the latest Sinatra project, Wilder wrote a series of short pieces for an album by the guitarist Mundell Lowe that follow in the tradition of the octets.[40] Their titles alone betray their ancestry:

"Suggestion for Bored Dancers"
"She Never Wore Makeup"
"What Happened Last Night?"
"Walk Softly"
"Let's Get Together and Cry"
"Mama Never Dug This Scene"
"Pop, What's a Passacaglia?"
"No Plans"
"The Endless Quest"
"Around the World in 2:34"
"An Unrelenting Memory"
"Tacet for Neurotics"

Likewise does the scoring recall the earlier pieces, now for a septet of flute, oboe, clarinet, bassoon, trumpet, and two French horns, accompanied by a rhythm section (although no harpsichord this time). In familiar fashion, the music flirts with and defies conventional standards of style and gesture, savoring the incongruity of a jazzy harmony or rhythm emanating from an oboe, bassoon, or French horn. Indeed, most of the pieces are firmly rooted in jazz and depend primarily on instrumentation to reference concert-music traditions. "Tacet for Neurotics" brings to mind the title of one of the first octets, "Neurotic Goldfish," but the new piece lacks the sense of stylistic dialogue of the earlier one. It is a more direct descendant of older "frenzy" pieces such as John Kirby's "Rehearsin' for a Nervous Breakdown" (1938) and Raymond Scott's "Bumpy Weather over Newark" (1939). Marian McPartland has noticed that the musical ideas in "Mama Never Dug This Scene" reemerged about ten years later in the lead cut ("Matrix") on Chick Corea's second album as leader, *Now He Sings, Now He Sobs* (1968). "Alec didn't believe me until I played 'Matrix' for him," wrote McPartland. "Then he was amazed and I think secretly delighted that he had the idea first."[41]

But the Mundell Lowe album also includes true hybrids, resting right in the center of the continuum. "Pop, What's a Passacaglia?" infuses an age-old variation form with the rhythmic informalities and backing sounds of swing, like dressing a stodgy old professor in a zoot suit. In "What Happened Last Night?" syncopated rhythms in 4/4 meter in the wind instruments nod to concert-music practices of Bartók or Stravinsky, but this is belied by the swung rhythms, the sounds of the electric guitar in the mix, and the brushes on a drum in the background (Example 11). "The Endless Quest," "Around the World in 2:34," and "An Unrelenting Memory" also take rhythms, chords, and melodic figures commonly heard in concert music and place them in uncharacteristic frames.

In these pieces, Wilder provocatively tests the limits and assumptions of musical style. He leads thoughtful listeners to ask exactly what style is, how it is created, and what it signifies. Such questions still left listeners confused, more than fifteen years after the octets first appeared. On the one hand, the Mundell Lowe album was chosen by the *New York Times* (November 18, 1956) as one of the "Best Jazz LPs of 1956." On the other hand, Wilder remembers reading reviews of the album that were "excoriating," on the grounds that the pieces were not jazz, "although no claim had been made that they were" (*Life Story*, 166). Whatever genre they typified, they were consistent with the general momentum of his work during the 1950s, toward building on his roughly three decades of experience with music of different traditions and establishing a distinctive compositional voice.

They were also another instance of connecting the personal and professional: Wilder recalls that some of the musical ideas for the Mundell Lowe pieces first appeared in music he wrote for the Sunday-afternoon gatherings in Stony Point. The act of recycling was itself a rarity for Wilder. He wrote: "And that's the only time in my life I have ever re-worked any material. I don't believe in it. It smacks of the kind of ego which presumes that every effort is a worthy one and mustn't be set aside. I believe in music for use. If it has had its use, move on, invent new things" (*Life Story*, 137). At the same time, the reuse of personal connections, the

Example 11: "What Happened Last Night?" mm. 44–46, condensed score (concert pitch)

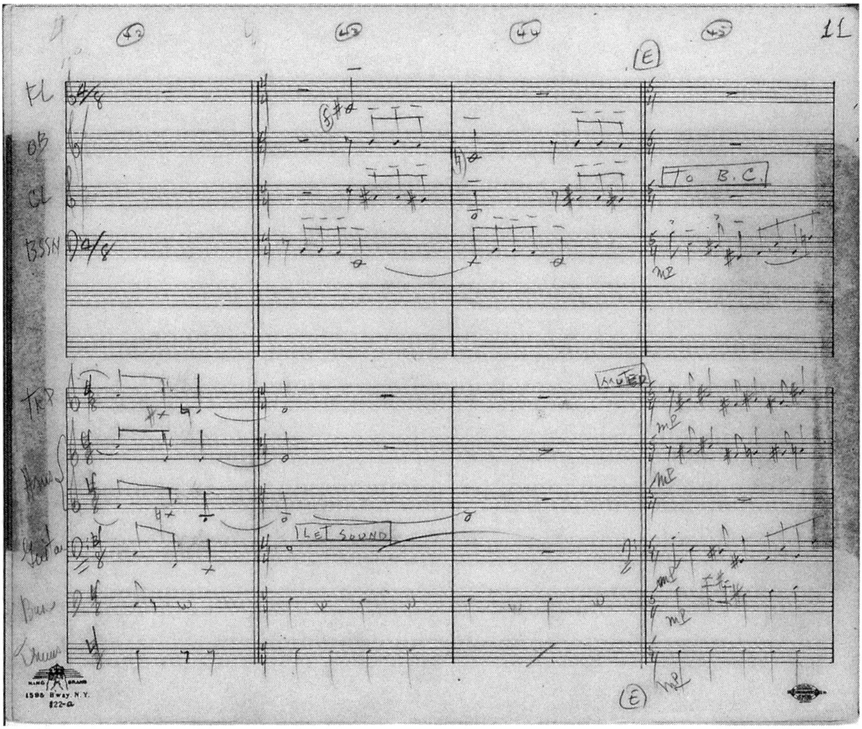

A page from Wilder's pencil score for "What Happened Last Night?" (The last measure is the first measure of Example 11.) (*TRO Archive*)

preservation of friendships within the musical community, had become a modus operandi. One of his most important and enduring musical affiliations had begun a few years before the Mundell Lowe album, when John Barrows introduced him to his colleagues in the New York Woodwind Quintet, the flutist Samuel Baron, the oboist Jerome Roth, the clarinetist David Glazer, and the bassoonist Bernard Garfield. Barrows had joined the group in 1952 and would remain its primary hornist until moving west to join the faculty of the University of Wisconsin at Madison in 1961. During that time, Wilder wrote six multi-movement woodwind quintets for the group (see "Selected Works," section VI) plus a set of popular song arrangements, *Alec Wilder Sketches the World's Most Beautiful Girls* (1955), a Solo Suite (1956), and suites for woodwinds and percussion based on his rescoring of James Sibley Watson's film *The Fall of the House of Usher* (1954) and on *Alice in Wonderland* (1958). He also sometimes tagged along with the group when they went on tour, and in summers in the late 1950s he accompanied them during annual six-week residencies at the University of Wisconsin at Milwaukee, sharing living quarters in a large house on the shore of Lake Michigan.[42]

Wilder's first work for the quintet was actually a set of arrangements of pieces by Henry Purcell, C. P. E. Bach, and Dietrich Buxtehude, which the group used frequently to open concerts.[43] Given that audiences of school children often asked them if they played jazz, the quintet asked Wilder for an original work with jazzy elements, and he wrote a light scherzo. When this too proved to be a success, Wilder used it as the third movement and cornerstone of his first Quintet for Woodwinds, which was premiered by the New York Woodwind Quintet at Carnegie Hall on February 17, 1954.[44] To create the other movements of the work, he used musical ideas from the scherzo as a springboard. The first and fourth are essentially fantasies on the main three-note motive of the scherzo, initially stripping away its jazzy connotations, treating it freely and contrapuntally, and later placing it back in the context of jazz. The second movement includes a brief reference to the third. The work in its entirety is uncommonly cohesive, not only a collection of movements in complementary tempos but also a web of musical interconnections. It was a conception of a multimovement work to which Wilder would repeatedly return, in some form or another, over the next twenty-odd years.

His first woodwind quintet launched a whole new focus for his work, on chamber music of modest proportions, written for musicians with whom he had close personal connections. Much of it was recorded and released on Golden Crest records, thanks to the efforts of Wilder's ardent supporter Clark F. Galehouse. A few distinctive features can be expected to appear in essentially all of these works: long, flowing melodies with irregular phrasing; extensive repetition and development of a handful of simple musical ideas, within or among movements (or both); a strong presence of counterpoint, either free or in the form of a fugato or canon; moments of whimsy arising from playful rhythms or quirky juxtapositions or denials of expectations; and a strong sense of warmth and sincerity, a bare rawness of emotion and sentiment, as if transporting the close personal feelings between composer and performers out through the air to the audience. These pieces may have moments of jazz flavoring—perhaps a melodic figure with blues elements, or an occasional chord type not ordinarily heard in concert halls, or a rhythm hinting at ragtime or swing—but just as common are entire movements conceived without a trace of stylistic mixture or hybridization. In one sense, Wilder's chamber movements are counterparts to the octets, with roots on opposite ends of the stylistic continuum. The octets, however, are much more likely to move toward and explore the center. Wilder's major works for small ensembles or soloists—the woodwind and brass

An early LP of Wilder's music on Golden Crest Records, featuring his Second Woodwind Quintet, Solo Suite, and various arrangements for woodwind quintet. The composer is pictured along with the personnel of the New York Woodwind Quintet: Samuel Baron, flute; Jerome Roth, oboe; John Barrows, French horn; Bernard Garfield, bassoon; and David Glazer, clarinet.

quintets and solo sonatas—often stay on the classical end and avoid any sense of crossover entirely, or offer only modest or occasional hints in that direction. They are less likely to embrace true hybridization.

A blues-flavored theme that arrives in the first movement of Wilder's second woodwind quintet (1956), for example, sounds like a visitor (upper staff of Example 12a).[45] It is a welcome guest, to be sure, not an interloper, but a visitor nonetheless. Aside from that theme, the music of the first movement rests squarely within the traditions of concert music, along the lines of his previous orchestral writing, with echoes of Debussy and Poulenc. Something similar happens in the second movement, when the theme reappears in the bassoon and French horn, accompanied by rich jazz harmonies (Example 12b). Eventually, however, as the theme returns in the remaining two movements, it undergoes a stylistic transformation. (It does keep its blue note.) The third movement begins with a true hybrid sound, but when the earlier theme returns, its rhythms have been completely straightened out (Example 12c). By the time we hear the theme one last time in the French horn near the end of the fourth movement, its rhythms remain straight, accompanied by angular, often dissonant figures in flute, clarinet, and bassoon (Example 12d). The theme's progress over the course of the four movements resembles the composer's own professional journey, from the night club to the concert hall.

When true hybrids do appear in Wilder's chamber music of the 1950s, they are more likely to be found in less traditional sorts of pieces. The Solo Suite for woodwind quintet (1956), for example, consists of five movements featuring each of the group's members in turn, with titles like "Scherzo for Flute: Jumpin' at the Wren House" and "Buffoonery for Bassoon: Bassooner or Later." The musical language wanders toward the stylistic center in all five movements, especially the fourth, featuring the French horn ("Blues for Horn: To the Manner Born"). Even more unusual is *Alec Wilder Sketches the World's Most Beautiful Girls* (1955), a collection of arrangements of love-soaked popular songs for woodwind quintet (Golden Crest CR-3026). Wilder arranged most of the songs to preserve the original tunes and harmonies but straighten out their rhythms, as if attempting to "dress them up" for the concert hall (e.g., "A Pretty Girl Is Like a Melody," "Have You Met Miss Jones"). It was, in other words, a counterpart of an approach he had taken early in his career, when he made swing arrangements of concert music, as if changing Bach out of his formal attire (see chapter 1). But a few of the *Sketches* move the quintet all the way to the other side of the spectrum, essentially reconceiving a dance-band chart for woodwinds ("The Girl on the Magazine Cover," "Mah Lindy Lou"), and some playfully draw from both traditions in roughly equal proportions ("Honeysuckle Rose," "Sleepytime Gal"). True to form, Wilder was equally comfortable at any place on the continuum.

As important as his first compositions for small ensembles during the 1950s were his earliest works for solo instruments and piano (see "Selected Works," section VI). Of course, given the influential role John Barrows played in Wilder's life and music, it is no surprise that his initial explorations of this genre were his first two Horn Sonatas (1954, 1957) and a five-movement Suite for Horn and Piano (1956). Stylistically, these works follow the same pattern as the quintets: the more formally titled sonatas are firmly rooted in classical traditions, while the suite has a freer language borrowing liberally from jazz. The second movement of the first sonata does venture outside of the classical sphere, but this is in the

Example 12: Excerpts from Woodwind Quintet No. 2 (all at concert pitch)
a. first movement, mm. 59–62, French horn and bassoon
b. second movement, mm. 44–46 (condensed score)
c. third movement, mm. 41–44, flute, oboe, bassoon
d. fourth movement, mm. 69–71

spirit of "concert jazz," like Gershwin's *Rhapsody in Blue* or Concerto in F. Otherwise, the two sonatas are classically conceived, with cyclic thematic returns in final movements and a harmonic language influenced by Milhaud and Poulenc and (especially) Hindemith. The suite, however, wanders freely over the stylistic spectrum and is generally lighter and more playful, as if reaching out to a certain group of listeners who do not normally pay much attention to French-horn music.

Wilder had Barrows to thank not only for inspiration and encouragement but also for his excellent recording of the two sonatas and suite with the pianist Milton Kaye (Golden Crest RE-7002 [1960]). Barrows had further helped Wilder make personal connections within classical-music circles that would boost his productivity for years to come: the more friends he had, the more opportunities he would find to get his music performed. Through Barrows he came to know the tubist Harvey Phillips, and the result was not only another lasting friendship but also Wilder's first tuba sonata (1959) and the first of many brass quintets, written for Phillips's group, the New York Brass Quintet (1959). Then came an alto-saxophone sonata for Donald Sinta (1960), a cello sonata for David Soyer (1961), a double-bass sonata for Gary Karr (1961), a flute sonata for Don Hammond (1961), and a trombone sonata for John Swallow (1961). Wilder began to develop a reputation among connoisseurs of the solo-recital repertoire that would match that of one of his compositional role models, Paul Hindemith, and that would rival Wilder's stature within the realm of commercial songwriting and recording. Of these years, Wilder later recalled: "I was busy writing, happy to know more and more superb players, and less than depressed because of the affection and respect of John Barrows and later the fortress of Harvey Phillips. . . . I was eager to entertain and amuse, to share the shade of a musical elm, to comment on the state of my soul rather than to set to music a manifesto of the downtrodden or to bring offerings to the altar of science, mathematics, or, aleatorily, anarchy" (*Life Story*, 149–51). He was, in other words, thoroughly and increasingly content with the direction his career had taken by the end of the 1950s, with the friendships he had formed, and with an artistic point of view that was both unapologetically self-effacing and stubbornly original.

4 Loyalties

The Prolific 1960s

IN NOVEMBER 1972, Alec Wilder wrote a reflective essay for the *New York Times* about the state of music at the end of a tumultuous decade.[1] "My particular complaint about rock," he explained, "is its continuing amateur point of view. For while amateurs can produce miracles, they can do it only once." Wilder wrote that he had witnessed remarkable professionalism in students at traditional music schools and colleges all over America, but that their efforts were seldom publicized, that they were "too calm, too quiet, and too civilized to constitute good copy." Rock musicians with "no destination" were getting all the attention. He was extolling the values and perspectives he had developed for himself when he was a music student about forty-five years earlier, well aware that American popular culture had long since passed him by. He had once worked comfortably, prodigiously, in the musical vanguard, challenging conventional preconceptions while mastering popular styles. Now, in the wake of the Beatles and Bob Dylan and Woodstock, he could only muse about the cultural transformation and fear for its future. "By . . . the early sixties, the world had begun its disintegration," he wrote in a memoir. "Joy, laughter, innocence, compassion, style, discipline, excellence, humility, [and] perspective were not only being choked off but even derided" (*The Search*, 102).

The crisis did not dampen Wilder's creative spirit but strengthened his commitment to his core principles. Continuing to follow trends he had begun at the end of the preceding decade, he wrote volumes of concert music for groups of all sizes in the 1960s, for wind ensembles and chamber orchestras and small groups and soloists with piano. He also wrote piano music, dramatic music of diverse kinds, and a handful of new songs, following traditional popular or art-song models. That none of this music followed prevailing fashions was a point of pride: "I was quite aware that I was outside the mainstream of successful music and musicians in both [popular and classical] areas of writing" (*Life Story*, 148). Indeed, he actively avoided recognition and publicity. "My only needs," he wrote, "were to compose, to see people I loved, admired, and trusted, to read, to make up puzzles, and occasionally to take a train ride" (*Life Story*, 150).

Also extending earlier trends, Wilder's loyalties to his artistic and ideological roots found musical expression through the efforts of loyal friends. After John Barrows joined the faculty of the University of Wisconsin in 1961, Wilder was increasingly inclined to take train rides to Madison, one of several destinations where he began developing new professional affiliations with admirers who were eager to play his music and introduce him to still more performers and potential dedicatees. As his travels and residencies and friendships multiplied, so did his catalog of original compositions perfectly suited for a faculty ensemble or senior recital or informal gathering in a college practice room or dormitory basement. The lifestyle clearly agreed with him: amid frequently changing scenery, he could find ample opportunities for writing music, usually with a promise of a performance, and develop warm personal relationships without overstaying his welcome.

Concert Works for Large Groups

One result of his increasing affiliations with school groups was a shift from writing for orchestra to writing for wind ensemble. His initial pull in this direction arose from a longtime friendship with the wind-ensemble pioneer Frederick Fennell and ongoing connections with his hometown music school:

> I heard Dr. Fennell and the Eastman School. He created the Eastman Woodwind Ensemble [*sic*], and I heard them either rehearsing or playing a perfectly marvelous piece by Persichetti. I think it was the Wind Symphony. I was so stoned by the sounds that came out of that group that I thought the idea terrified me, because of all the keys in which you'd have to write. I'd never written for baritone horn. I'd never written for a lot of those instruments. The idea of working with such an enormous amalgam of sounds really petrified me. But I was compelled to do it because of the richness of it all. Dr. Fennell had been a friend of mine for many years, so I went ahead and wrote a five-movement piece for him and had a lot of fun with it.[2]

Wilder was being modest. His years of experience as a composer and arranger had given him a deep understanding of instruments and transpositions, even if he had never actually written a part for a baritone horn or euphonium. But he was understandably intrigued, if not intimidated, by the rich sound of wind instruments with more than one player per part, plus a percussion battery that could be much expanded over the traditional orchestra section.

The five-movement piece he wrote for Fennell became the first in a series of works for large groups with the title "Entertainment" (see "Selected Works," section VII). This title, Wilder explained, was a response to the earnest seriousness he had noticed in other music of the era, in which "entertainment is taboo," the "concert hall has become the lecture hall," and "everything in art as well as life must be solemn and 'important.'" He came to agree with one of his stylistic forebears, Maurice Ravel: "I remember someone telling me of attending a *soirée* in Paris at which Maurice Ravel was present. My friend overheard a man being offensive to Monsieur Ravel by suggesting to him that he was trying to become a successor to some recently deceased great composer. My friend heard Ravel reply, 'No Monsieur, you are wrong. I am simply trying to entertain'" (*Life Story*, 168).

Ultimately, Wilder would write seven multimovement Entertainments for wind ensemble or orchestra, or soloist with orchestra, between 1960 and 1975. The music in them is consistently witty and playful and begs not to be taken too seriously. Elements of jazz, such as chord structures or progressions, or bluesy melodic inflections, or even just a drumstick keeping a beat on a ride cymbal, figure prominently throughout the pieces and contribute to their aura of informality or playfulness.

The Entertainments are, in other words, artistic successors to the octets. Both series often share a lighthearted sensibility and blend classical and jazz idioms with comparable dexterity. Entertainment No. 1 (1960), for example, starts with a series of motivic pronouncements that seem to belong in a cartoon soundtrack, recalling some of the original inspirations for the octets such as Raymond Scott, but then it eventually settles into a groove that draws equally from different traditions. Over a repeating syncopated chord pattern, with harmonies taken directly from the jazz playbook (Example 13a), we hear a melody in straight rhythms that has few jazz elements at all (Example 13b). This is just the kind of hybrid sound that Wilder had made his signature, especially after the second set of octets and the pieces for Mundell Lowe. The second movement of Entertainment No. 1 brings back a primary motive from the first but is mostly rooted on the classical end of the stylistic continuum, as if following, or responding to, concert-band traditions in the music of Paul Hindemith or William Schuman or Vincent Persichetti. Then the third

Example 13: Excerpts from Entertainment No. 1, first movement (at concert pitch) a. m. 54, saxophones and trombones b. mm. 56–58, B♭ clarinet (concert pitch, doubled 8va by flute and E♭ clarinet)

movement builds on this premise further, with a mock-serious motive that ultimately becomes absorbed in playful contrapuntal lines. When the fourth movement begins, a sternly conceived fugato suggests a full commitment to concert-music traditions, until it gives way to what sounds like an interlude for dance band; the contrasting styles continue their dialogue until the movement's end. In the fifth-movement finale, the notion of hybrid is back, in grand Gershwinesque gestures (punctuated by strident thwacks from the percussion section, which includes a section of steel I-beam dropped on the floor), followed by music with roots in a jazz ballad and then reminiscences of the fairly stiff principal motive and cartoonish filigrees first heard when the entire piece began. As is often the case in Wilder's initial efforts in a certain genre or medium, the work exudes freshness and vitality, like an explorer who is eager to share a new discovery.

But the Entertainments are entertaining not only because of their interplay of styles and traditions. They are much more than a new set of octets with expanded instrumentation. They call upon all the lessons Wilder had learned in his sundry musical experiences over three decades, about instrumental colors, formal rhetoric, and the craft of composition. Within the melodic layering and fugatos of the third and fourth movements of Entertainment No. 1—also the first movement of No. 2 and the third movement of No. 3, among many others—is the work of a skilled contrapuntist. At some point in the late 1950s and early 1960s, as he was devoting more and more of his time to concert music, Wilder also began to experiment with melodies having a high variety of different pitches, up to eleven or sometimes all twelve of the notes of the chromatic scale in some meaningful ordering, with few or no repetitions. A twelve-note theme in the fourth movement of Entertainment No. 2 (1966), for example, exhausts the total chromatic by alternating notes of an expanding chromatic wedge pattern (Example 14a). In the first movement of Entertainment No. 5 (1969), the chromatic resource is fully presented with a greater degree of rhythmic and intervallic variety (Example 14b). Wilder never took the full plunge into the twelve-tone method—his pitch-saturated formulations are just melodies, not "tone rows" providing source material for both melody and harmony—but he did occasionally build formal structures based on restatements of pitch-saturated themes at different levels of transposition (e.g., the first movement of Entertainment No. 5; also the Variations movement of the *Sand Castles* Suite [1961]). Generally speaking, if the Entertainments leave an impression of being light or innocuous, it is because Wilder has planned and crafted that impression with skill and care, not because he lacked focus or ambition when he created them.

Wilder's other works for large ensembles in the 1960s all use the group as backdrop for a soloist in a concerto or suite (see "Selected Works," section VII). In every case, of course, he wrote with a specific soloist in mind, including old friends such as John Barrows (the second Horn Concerto [1960]; Air for Horn and Small Wind Ensemble [1963]) and Harvey Phillips (Concerto for Tuba and Wind Ensemble [1968]), and new ones such as Donald Sinta (Concerto for Alto Saxophone and Wind Ensemble [1966]) and Clark Terry (Concerto No. 2 for Trumpet/Flugelhorn and Wind Ensemble [1969]). Each piece has a story behind it. The saxophonist Stan Getz had played the Wilder/Sundgaard song "Where

Example 14: Themes from Entertainments with high note variety
a. Entertainment No. 2, fourth movement, mm. 1–2, violins and violas
b. Entertainment No. 5, first movement, mm. 1–4, trombones

Do You Go?" at his mother's funeral and arranged to meet Wilder through their mutual friends Jackie Cain and Roy Kral (*Life Story*, 171–74). At Getz's request, Wilder wrote two multimovement pieces for him: the Suite No. 1 for Tenor Saxophone and Strings (1963), which Getz premiered with Arthur Fiedler and the Boston Pops at Tanglewood in 1966, and a Concerto for Tenor Saxophone and Chamber Orchestra (1968), which Getz was scheduled to perform at Chautauqua but did not properly prepare, yielding instead to an alcoholic binge. The trumpeter and *Tonight Show* bandleader Doc Severinsen also failed to perform, or even to acknowledge receiving, a concerto Wilder wrote for him (Concerto No. 1 for Trumpet and Wind Ensemble [1967]; *Life Story*, 170–71). Wilder had better luck with the Suite No. 2 for Tenor Saxophone and Strings that he wrote for Zoot Sims, who premiered it at the University of Wisconsin in 1966.[3] Two years later, Sims also premiered the concerto Wilder had written for Stan Getz, with the University of Miami Symphonic Wind Ensemble conducted by Frederick Fennell.[4]

For the most part, there is a difference in style between the solo pieces Wilder wrote for friends from the classical world and those he wrote for jazz artists. The pieces tailored for John Barrows and Harvey Phillips and Donald Sinta follow Wilder's familiar practices, moving smoothly between typical concert-hall styles and passages of hybrid. The pieces for Stan Getz and Zoot Sims and Clark Terry, however, are more consistently rooted in jazz. When crossover elements occur in these works, the interface is less smooth, more in the rhetoric of dialogue or juxtaposition. The fugato at the beginning of the second movement of the Suite No. 2 for Tenor Saxophone and Strings (written for Zoot Sims) is a surprising presence amid jazz riffs and ballad-like melodies. The first movement of the Concerto for Tenor Saxophone and Chamber Orchestra (written for Stan Getz) begins with a conspicuously staid twelve-tone theme that recurs like a fugue subject, in whole and in fragmentation and at different transpositions; elsewhere in the piece are pure jazz harmonies and a jazz waltz. And the finale of the Concerto No. 2 for Trumpet/Flugelhorn and Wind Ensemble (written for Clark Terry), quite unlike the other movements, mostly avoids the language of jazz entirely.

Chamber Music

The most intense focus of Wilder's work in the 1960s fell on music for small groups of instruments, from solo pieces and brass and woodwind quintets to chamber ensembles of as many as nineteen performers. These works were mostly intended for private study or performance in relatively intimate settings, such as rehearsal studios or recital halls. Those that have traditional instrumentations and carry historically standard titles—the brass or woodwind quintets, the sonatas for solo instruments with piano—are more likely to follow familiar formatting conventions and to be more firmly rooted in the style of traditional concert music. They are likely to have four movements, following nineteenth-century practice, with customary tempo relationships. Works for more unusual combinations, often with the title of "suite," are less predictably structured and are likely to mix stylistic elements more liberally. Their numbers of movements and tempo relationships are typically idiosyncratic and widely variable. In a third category are large collections of short pieces for two to four players that Wilder wrote sporadically over a period of years, perfectly suited for a group of students in a practice room.

The woodwind and brass quintets build on a legacy that began with Wilder's shift toward concert music in the 1950s. Because of John Barrows's relocation to the University of Wisconsin in 1961, however, Wilder stopped writing exclusively for the New York Woodwind Quintet and developed a close relationship with Barrows's new group in Madison, the Wingra Quintet.[5] Some of the five woodwind quintets he wrote between 1964 and 1971 (Nos. 7–11) were written for the Wingra, or for other quintets elsewhere in the United States. (Quintet No. 8, written for a student group at the University of Wisconsin, was subtitled "Suite for Non-Voting Quintet.") Likewise did Wilder end his close affiliation with the New York Brass Quintet after Harvey Phillips left the group to become an administrator at the New England Conservatory in 1967. Wilder's two brass quintets from this decade, numbered 2 and 3, show his response to the changing times: the second, from 1961, has the same stiff formality and intermovement connections found in some of the earlier woodwind quintets, while the third, dated 1970, is more complex and adventurous and even experiments some with rock idioms (in the third movement).

In the pages of Wilder's other music for chamber ensembles from the 1960s are a full accounting of his interests, tendencies, and affiliations (see "Selected Works," section VIII). He wrote for groups of woodwinds, groups of brass, and various unusual combinations, their instrumentations dictated, as always, by a connection to a particular musician or ensemble. For students at the University of Wisconsin he wrote the Suite for Four Bassoons (1965). For Emory Remington and his students at Eastman he wrote the Suite for Nineteen Trombones (1967). For Gerry Mulligan and John Barrows he wrote a Suite for Baritone Saxophone, Horn, and Woodwind Quintet (1966). A few years after that, he wrote a second similar piece for Mulligan, the Suite for Baritone Saxophone, Woodwind Sextet, Bass, and Drums (1971). For Gary Karr he wrote a Suite for String Bass and Guitar

At the Eastman School of Music in 1971, with bass trombonist Donald Knaub, pianist Barry Snyder, and composer Samuel Adler. (*Louis Ouzer*)

(1968). Even so, pieces were not always premiered by the performer(s) for whom they were written. The suite for Gerry Mulligan was actually premiered by Glenn Bowen along with John Barrows and the New York Woodwind Quintet (in Milwaukee on July 11, 1966).[6] Wilder apparently never heard the piece for trombone choir, which Remington found difficult to conduct (*Life Story*, 168–69), although Gary Karr both premiered and recorded the pieces Wilder wrote for him.[7]

It comes as no surprise to find styles in these works falling anywhere on the spectrum, for brief passages or for entire movements and through any conceivable means, from instrumental shadings to melodic inflections to hybrid harmonies and rhythms. A Saxophone Quartet (1963) sounds like an homage to earlier French composers, Debussy, Ravel, and Poulenc, while the works for Mulligan draw most directly from jazz traditions, similar to the solo pieces for Stan Getz and Zoot Sims. A Nonet for Brass Ensemble (1969) comes across as a sequel to the earlier *Jazz Suite* for French-horn quartet and rhythm section (1951). By this time, however, in the wake of shifting tastes and cultural transformations, Wilder's stylistic eclecticism was hardly unique. In 1957, Gunther Schuller had described a "third stream" in American music, merging cultivated and vernacular traditions, looking back to music of Red Norvo, George Handy, and Wilder, among others.[8] In the 1960s, Schuller himself helped to popularize third-stream principles in works such as Concertino for Jazz Quartet and Orchestra (1960), and the trend had developed in music such as Jimmy Giuffre's "Three We" (on the album *Free Fall* [1962]) and Larry Austin's *Improvisations for Orchestra and Jazz Soloists* (1967). Only the role of improvisation separates Wilder's practice from much third-stream music. Most of his scores are fully notated; he said that he preferred to "control the material."[9] Otherwise, he was fully committed to the movement's celebration of a wide array of cultural forces and influences, and he surely watched with amusement as beliefs he had held for decades began to find a vibrant currency.

The one new interest that emerged in Wilder's chamber music in the late 1960s undoubtedly grew out of his extensive experience in the studios, hallways, and rehearsal halls of music schools and college music departments, including a semester as composer-in-residence at the University of Wisconsin in the winter of 1968 (*Life Story*, 95, 174, 176–77). For students, colleagues, and friends, he began writing a large number of short pieces, most of them concise explorations of a single compositional premise. Many such miniatures were eventually collected together, yielding the Twelve Duets for Horn and Bassoon (1967), the ten-movement Suite for Four Horns (1968), the Twenty-Two Duets for Two Horns (1968), the Seven Duets for Horn and Bassoon (1969), and the Suite (Ten Duets) for Tubas (1970).[10] Wilder seized the opportunity when writing these pieces to focus his efforts as he rarely had before, to explore an extreme of economy and concision. They became a compositional laboratory for testing ideas or trying out previously unexplored techniques. As John Barrows wrote in the preface to the Twenty-Two Duets, the collections also contain "subtle humor, an occasional joke, and just plain good fun."[11]

These short pieces offer, in other words, a most revealing glimpse into Alec Wilder's musical state of mind as he reached his sixtieth birthday in 1967. Of course, the collections have ample instances of stylistic amalgams, jocular parodies, and motivic saturations. As in some of his music for larger groups, they also display a keen interest in orderings of a complete or near-complete chromatic collection, as if contemplating a turn toward the twelve-tone method. (If so, it was never more than a contemplation.) But what especially drew his interest in these collections was counterpoint, chiefly the technique of canon. Nine of the twenty-two horn duets, for example, are completely canonic from beginning to end. The answering voice usually enters at a one- or two-bar distance and usually is not transposed. And while the cerebral nature of canonic construction may seem inconsistent with Wilder's general reliance on intuition and expressive impulse in the compositional process—and with his oft-expressed opposition to musical intellectualism—they are completely consistent with a whole other side of his personality, his interest in games and puzzles. His friend James Maher has recalled Wilder spending countless hours during creative dry spells doing nothing but constructing crossword puzzles.[12] A canon is a puzzle to be solved, a complex of rules and restrictions challenging a composer to produce a musical, artistically satisfying result. Collected together with other pieces of similar lengths, perhaps a little jazz waltz or a burst of instrumental wizardry or a simple tune built on an infectious motivic figure, they constitute a full accounting of the composer and his creative interests.

Wilder had been interested in fugue since his contrapuntal studies with Herbert Inch at Eastman in the late 1920s. He had incorporated fugatos into two movements of his early string quartet (early 1930s) and had written a jazz fugue for one of the octets ("Sea Fugue Mama" [1939]). Several movements of the woodwind quintets from the 1950s are likewise fugal, as are passages from the third and fourth movements of Entertainment No. 1 (1960). But strict canon is a relative newcomer to Wilder's compositional methods, certainly a throwback to the very beginnings of his lessons with Inch. His first extensive canonic writing in a major concert work appeared in the Sonata for Clarinet and Piano, written in 1963 for Glenn Bowen, a colleague of John Barrows on the University of Wisconsin faculty. Bowen was also pursuing a doctorate at Eastman and would eventually write a dissertation about the clarinet in Wilder's chamber music.[13] The sonata is a contrapuntal showpiece, with several extended canonic passages and frequent moments of interweaving melodies. A two-voice canon in the third movement occurs atop a jazz-flavored chord pattern (Example 15a). Unusually for Wilder, the answering voice (piano right hand) is transposed, first up a minor third from the leading voice (clarinet), later up a major second. Virtually all of Wilder's many other canons throughout his work do not include transpositions, as in the treatment of a twelve-tone theme in the sonata's fourth movement (Example 15b). When the music of the sonata is not contrapuntal, it occupies a customary range around the center of the stylistic continuum, with clear debts to Gershwin.

Some sort of contrapuntal focus, often a passage of extensive canon, became a trademark of Wilder's chamber music for solo instruments in the 1960s (see "Selected Works," section IX). He would eventually write at least one solo sonata for almost every orchestral instrument, starting with the first horn sonata in 1953 (see chapter 3) and extending to the third horn sonata in 1970. The violin is notably absent from the series. Wilder explained, "There have been too damn many mag-

Example 15: Excerpts from the Clarinet Sonata (all at concert pitch) a. third movement, mm. 43–46 b. fourth movement, mm. 16–19

nificent pieces written for violin, and unless I could write an undramatic sonata, I'd rather omit it."[14] He also acknowledged that he wrote no solo sonatas for the harp ("couldn't face" it) or bass clarinet ("not enough dynamic range"). And yet he did write solo sonatas for easily overlooked members of the orchestral family, the bass trombone (1969) and English horn (undated), and for instruments more closely associated with wind ensembles, the alto saxophone (1960) and euphonium (1968). With the sonata series, he found ample new performers for his music, including the dedicatees Don Hammond (flute, 1961), John Swallow (trombone, 1961; euphonium, 1968), Joe Wilder (trumpet, 1963), Karen Tuttle (viola, 1965), and George Roberts (bass trombone, 1969).

Wilder's close friendship with Harvey Phillips gave rise to a number of new works for tuba, spearheading a revolution in the repertoire for that instrument. As Phillips remarked (according to Wilder) after his initial reading of Wilder's first tuba sonata (1959), with the pianist Milton Kaye: "Well, that's the third"—recognizing that Vaughan Williams's Concerto (1954) and Hindemith's Sonata (1955) now had a companion on the short list of major works for tuba (*Life Story*, 162). In subsequent years Wilder would compose the "Effie" Suite for tuba, vibraphone, and drums (children's album, 1959), a duo suite for Phillips and the bassist Gary Karr with piano (1962), two duo suites for Phillips and John Barrows (1963, 1971), three suites for tuba and piano (Nos. 2, 3, and 4) in honor of Phillips's children (1964, 1966, 1968), a concerto for tuba and wind ensemble (1968), a short "Song for Carol" in honor of Phillips's wife (1968), three suites for solo tuba (collected together as the eighteen-movement *Convalescence Suite* [1971–75]), and a second solo sonata in honor of Phillips's mother (1975). Wilder shared Phillips's conviction that the tuba need not be typecast as a punctuator of snorting bass lines, and he made a strong effort to demonstrate the instrument's full expressive range, exploring and exploiting Phillips's virtuosic technique. Wilder also brought a range of ambitions to these works, composing everything from modest ditties to complex motivic designs and carefully crafted counterpoint.

A closer look at two of Wilder's major works for tuba offers a helpful overview of his contributions to the chamber-music genre at this point in his life. His sonata for tuba and piano (1959) is a formidable attempt to produce a pillar of the repertoire. Indeed, the first movement seems to draw inspiration from its towering predecessor, in open, mildly dissonant harmonies and quartal melodic lines that essentially pick up where Hindemith left off. Of course, there are moments of jazz flavoring in Wilder's harmonic language, but this too has precedents in Hindemith, in works such as the *Suite 1922* (1922) and the *Zeitoper Neues vom Tage* (1929).[15] Wilder's second movement then delves even deeper into popular idioms, with ragtime gestures and hints of swing infiltrating a classically conceived scherzo. The third and fourth movements likewise present Wilder's familiar blend of vernacular touches within overall conceptions rooted in the cultivated traditions, at times evoking not only Hindemith but also Prokofiev and Shostakovich. On the whole, the movements make complementary contributions to a cohesive artistic statement.

The fifth Suite for Tuba and Piano (1963), by contrast, is much more of a loose collection, in a lighter, more playful tone. It has four movements, like the sonata, but they are shorter and not as densely packed with musical invention. The Suite's first movement is a stroll through the meadow, in the piano's bouncy, oom-pah rhythms, while the tuba supplies only a lilting melody, never a rhythmic "oom." The second movement is a lyrical ballad, the third a brief scherzo; like the first, they each develop essentially one musical idea and then close just at the point when it is time to move on. The final movement adds something entirely different: a strict, thirty-seven-bar, three-voice canon completely in baroque style, as if completing an assignment for counterpoint class.[16] The suite is a tasting menu; the sonata is a four-course meal.

And so it goes for Wilder's many solo sonatas and suites and other chamber music and larger instrumental works of the 1960s (see "Selected Works," sections

VII, VIII, and IX). The personal comfort brought to him by an ever-growing network of friends and admirers yielded not only abundant opportunities for performances but also inspirational levels of professional satisfaction and self-confidence.

Songs for Everyone

In the swirl of creative winds blowing across Wilder's musical landscape in the early 1960s, songs are curiously rare. Seven excellent songs emerged from his score for Jerome Hill's film *Open the Door and See All the People* (1964), but these all began as instrumental underscoring, to which lyrics were added after the fact. The few originally conceived songs from this time include a collaboration with William Engvick ("I Like It Here" [1961]), another with Fran Landesman ("You're Free" [1961]), and an art-song setting of a poem by the nineteenth-century French poet Alfred de Musset, dedicated to Jerome Hill ("A. M. Victor Hugo" [1962]). These efforts mostly conform to songwriting practices Wilder had by this time thoroughly tested and perfected—"You're Free" has some unusual phrase imbalances ("breaking free" from conventions), which are especially evident in Anthony Newley's recording—but clearly Wilder's primary compositional interests lay elsewhere in the early years of the decade.[17]

What brought him back to the art of the song was a potential audience that had always been close to his heart: children. In 1964 and 1965, he and Engvick assembled *Lullabies and Night Songs*, a songbook directed toward young ears and sensibilities, with enchanting illustrations by Maurice Sendak.[18] The collection brings together forty-eight songs, in simple scoring and in accessible keys, most of them occupying only a single page. Some are simple arrangements of familiar tunes (such as "All through the Night," "Go Tell Aunt Rhody"), although others have lyrics of familiar songs presented with new or partially rewritten melodies (such as "All the Pretty Li'l Horses," "Rock-a-Bye, Baby"). A majority of them are settings of poems that are not normally known as songs—in other words, song settings—because, as the book's preface indicates, "they seem to ask to be sung as well as read." These include the poetry of William Blake ("Cradle Song"), James Thurber ("The Golux's Song," "Hark, Hark, the Dogs Do Bark"), Rudyard Kipling ("Seal Lullaby"), Robert Louis Stevenson ("Windy Nights"), and others, including some anonymous verse. The collection also includes a handful of songs from earlier projects (e.g., "Douglas Mountain," from *The Wind Blows Free*; "The Cuckoo Is a Pretty Bird," from *The Lowland Sea*), and a few with lyrics newly written by Engvick ("The Elephant Present," "The Journey," "Many Million Years Ago," "Where Do You Sleep?") or by Wilder ("The Telephone Book

Lullaby"). *Lullabies and Night Songs* has endured as a classic of its kind, preserved and revitalized by splendid recordings of many of the songs by Jan DeGaetani (1985) and by Heidi Grant Murphy (2009).[19]

Wilder's work on this project seems to have reignited a flame. As the 1960s wore on, he began gradually to return more and more to the song genre, even while continuing to write prodigious amounts of instrumental concert music. Art songs and popular songs appeared in roughly equal number in these years and may also have been created through similar processes of text setting, starting with a completed poem, as with many of the children's songs. The sources for the texts are likewise similar: art-song texts mostly came not from magazines or poetry anthologies but from friends, in the manner of a pop-song collaboration. The resulting musical settings, which Wilder usually had professionally copied, became gifts for those friends, just as a recently completed sonata would be a gift for the instrumentalist for whom it was composed.[20] Scores survive from these years for settings of poetry

An undated self-portrait. (*Alec Wilder Archive, Sibley Music Library, Eastman School of Music*)

by the record-company executive David Kapp ("One Small Voice") and by Percy Seitlin ("Something Is Up"), an author of some renown who based a character on Wilder in his book *Is Anything All Right?*[21] In a note to a copyist regarding his setting of a poem entitled "The Leaves Are Falling," Wilder asked that four copies of the finished score be sent to the band director at Ithaca (New York) High School, where the poet, Robbine Hockett, was apparently a student.

Wilder set at least four poems in the late 1960s by his friend Ethan Ayer, who was known as a novelist (*The Enclosure* [1951]) and as the librettist for Douglas Moore's opera *Wings of the Dove* (1961), an adaptation of Henry James's novel. (Wilder also dedicated his fifth Suite for Tuba and Piano to Ayer.) When Wilder's language in these songs is triadic or plain, as in "Snow Man" and "The Traveling Singer," they share traits with some of his efforts in the popular realm. When they are angular and dissonant and contrapuntal, however, as in "Lyric Found in a Bottle" and "The Idiot," they seem more akin to recent instrumental music. The primary accompanimental gestures in "The Idiot," for example, resemble music Wilder wrote for the fourth movement of his first tuba sonata (1959). The song features a pairing of contrapuntal lines in mostly contrary motion with occasional interruptions of parallel sixths or thirds (Example 16). Its melodic line sometimes doubles, sometimes complements the piano's counterpoint, especially bringing out lines of half steps ("He thought he would be") and whole steps ("-tu-ous he thought"). Fans of "I'll Be Around" and "While We're Young" may have a tough time hearing a song like "The Idiot" as a product of the same creative mind. It joins a whole different tradition of American song, far from Rodgers and Arlen, far even from the language of Wilder's earlier art songs, leaning more toward the modernist aesthetic of Charles Ives or Ruth Crawford Seeger.

At the same time, Wilder's popular songs from the late 1960s stay securely within traditions he had been following for decades. He wrote two more songs with Fran Landesman, "Photographs (Me in Love with You)" and "Walk Pretty," and one with William Engvick, "Lovers and Losers," that are classic exemplars of the thirty-two-bar AABA standard. They are also some of his most compelling work in the genre, evidence that he was at the top of his form as he entered his golden years. Of course, it helps that these songs have been so artfully performed in recordings by Teddi King, Marlene VerPlanck, Jackie and Roy, and Wesla Whitfield, among others.[22]

The one noteworthy pop song from this period that breaks out of the mold, "Night Talk," has a lyric by Wilder himself. With the freedom to control and adjust the structure of the text, he seems eager to experiment and go against expectations. As the music appears to follow the text, an art-song sensibility creeps in,

Example 16: "The Idiot," mm. 1–7

and indeed the classic recording of this song by Dick Haymes has the feel of a pop-song/art-song hybrid.[23] It begins with a lengthy verse:

When darkness shrouds the town
A loneliness steals down around your heart.
You bitterly reenact your defeats
As you restlessly wander on through the streets.
You see a familiar sign,
You remember the magic of wine,
So you drink a bit,
It revives your wit,
Your hungry heart yearns,
Your courage returns,
So you look about the place,
'Til you find a list'ning face, then,

The refrain continues to paint a dreary picture of dark solitude:

A Night talk,
That's when the ghosts walk,
That's when the past comes up and hits you,
And the warmth of the wine permits you
To relax with sweet forgotten facts and fancies.

A' Night talk,
Always seems right talk.
You can share a world that's gone
'Til the lonely glow of dawn.

B It's then when the room gets quiet,
It's useless for you to deny it,
You're as alone as before,
There's little but silence in store.
Lovely friend, it's the end of
Night talk.

Wilder referred to "Night Talk" as a "white version" of Billy Strayhorn's "Lush Life," an apt comparison with another song about a fruitless search for meaning in a lonely world.[24] Both songs also wander outside of formal conventions, finding signposts in primary motives but failing to project the clarity of an orderly, rational existence. In Wilder's case, the first hint of formal irregularity (after the meandering verse) happens in the last line of the A strain ("To relax . . ."), which extends the eight-bar section to twelve. Then the A strain begins again ("Night talk . . ."), but after eight bars—just at the point where the first A was extended—a new melody begins, the beginning of another lonely day ("It's then when the room gets quiet . . ."). This B strain starts with two couplets, like A, and adds a four-bar extension, also like A, except now the extension works its way back to the repetition of the song title as hook. We get the distinct impression that Wilder's scenario of pathetic misery is not fully a product of his imagination, that he is writing from poignant personal experience.

At some point in the late 1960s, Wilder also began to write pop songs with a new major collaborator, his third after William Engvick and Arnold Sundgaard. The relationship began earlier in the decade, when Loonis McGlohon, a musician and radio personality in Charlotte, North Carolina, contacted the composer for support with a local radio program devoted to Wilder's music.[25] After a personal meeting and a period of correspondence, McGlohon sent Wilder some songs he had written, asking for an appraisal. Wilder's reply was emphatic: "Where the hell have you been? I've been looking for you. . . . Send me a lyric."[26] They began writing songs together, sometimes by phone or mail, sometimes in person during one of Wilder's extended visits to McGlohon's home in North Carolina. The collaboration endured for the rest of Wilder's life, yielding a major cache of songs.[27]

One of their earliest collaborations was actually a group of songs for an Oz-oriented theme park in the North Carolina mountains.[28] The project was a brainchild of Jack Pentes, an artist and designer in Charlotte, with financial support from a pair of brothers, Harry and Grover Robbins, who had also built a tourist attraction, golf course, and ski resort in the area. The Land of Oz hosted groups of visitors for reenactments of Dorothy's journey at various points along the mountainside, starting with her simple farmhouse and the menacing cyclone, then following the Yellow Brick Road to the Emerald City. The characters that visitors met along the way sang Wilder-McGlohon songs to introduce themselves: first the Tin Man ("I Lost My Heart . . . and I Don't Know Where to Find It"), then the Scarecrow ("I'd Like to Have a Brain"), the Cowardly Lion ("I'm a Fraidy Cat"), and the Witch ("How Do I Brew This Stew?"). After the visitors reached the castle, the Wizard shared his wisdom in "Open Your Eyes" ("So open your eyes and reach for the world / But it's home, that's where you must start / To really see through eyes of love / And then you will learn the wisdom of the heart"). Then Dorothy sang Harold Arlen and Yip Harburg's "Over the Rainbow" to express her wishes to the wizard, an open acknowledgment of the unavoidable connections between Land of Oz and the classic film. Finally, as Dorothy floated away in her balloon, the most appealing Wilder-McGlohon song of the group, "The Wonderful Wizard of Oz," emanated from strategically placed speakers across the mountaintop (in a recording by Mary Mayo).[29] The song is a stylish jazz waltz, backed by a swing-era arrangement, summing up the whole experience ("Do you know another place scarecrows can dance? / And where else could you speak to a lion by chance? / Or see a man wearing aluminum pants? / In the Wonderful Land of Oz!"). The park was a popular attraction when it first opened in 1970 but fell out of favor and into disrepair and closed a decade later.[30]

Just as this project was getting off the ground, sometime in 1968, Wilder's interest in music for children was likewise sparked by an idea from a friend, Father Henry Atwell of St. Agnes church in Avon, New York, a few miles south of Rochester. When Atwell suggested that Wilder write a choral work on a topical subject for the late 1960s—peace—the composer imagined a text consisting entirely of the words of children. Atwell eventually collected around three hundred essays on the subject of peace from local children, age twelve and under, from which Wilder selected and adapted text for *Children's Plea for Peace*, a fourteen-minute cantata for children's chorus and wind ensemble. Wilder's opening narration captures the work's overall tone: "Here are the children. Here are their words and their voices. Here is how they feel about the world as they see it. They still play and laugh and misbehave, but they've begun to think of something that maybe children never thought about before: a peaceful world. They've heard of everything else—every frightening, monstrous thing—but peace. So here they are to sing, to speak of peace in their own puzzled, angry, innocent voices."

Choir members speak or sing excerpts from the essays over a lush instrumental bed that often features a simple recurring theme, in the same vein as Copland's *Lincoln Portrait* (1942). Wilder himself had done much the same thing a few years before the cantata in *Names from the War* (1960), showcasing a poem by Bruce Catton about the Civil War. This sort of writing was not, in any case, a challenging exercise for a composer experienced in commercial music and film scoring, and Wilder's writing in the cantata effectively complements and features touching declarations from the voices about peace and its polar opposite: "Peace is a big family of quietness"; "It would be wonderful to live without the fear you're going to be bombed"; and so forth.

Children's Plea for Peace was premiered in Avon on May 3, 1969, and in Rochester the next day, by a chorus from the Eastman Preparatory Division and members of the Eastman Wind Ensemble, conducted by the Eastman professor Milford Fargo and narrated by the Eastman composer Warren Benson.[31] Wilder was typically self-effacing about the music itself—"It was no great musical work"—but, he wrote, "everything surrounding it *was* great: the beautiful, beautiful children crocodiling across to the church from the school, the perfect spring day, the tender green of the budding leaves, the spring flowers, the friendly spirit of the congregation" (*Letters I Never Mailed*, 226). In this bucolic setting and surrounded by such innocence and sincerity, he reflected, "my cynicism and gloomy view of life seemed like an unwarrantable illness" (*The Search*, 112).

Alas, the American presence in Vietnam was far from over in 1969, and Wilder would find ample reasons to regain his cynicism in the years to come. At the same time, his worldview hardly prevented him from maintaining a furious pace of creative production, from finding abundant causes to celebrate or sentiments to express; perhaps he was escaping into his work. In any case, his instrumental and vocal compositions in the late 1960s shared time with theatrical ambitions, including an ill-fated stage adaptation of his and Hugh Martin's music for the *Grandma Moses* film.[32] A project that did reach fruition, a one-act opera with a libretto by Arnold Sundgaard called *The Opening*, is a Cinderella story told from the point of view of the audience, a return to the spirit and tone of two of his and Sundgaard's chamber operas from the 1950s, *Cumberland Fair* and *Sunday Excursion*. *The Opening* premiered on May 19, 1969, just sixteen days after the first performance of his children's cantata, at the New England Conservatory in Boston, thanks, no doubt, to the support of his good friends in the school's administration, president Gunther Schuller and vice president Harvey Phillips. His impact and influence, his web of admirers and advocates, continued to grow, and he still had plenty more to say.

5 Celebrations

Reflection and Reaffirmation in the 1970s

ALEC WILDER'S FINAL DECADE unfolded with recurring themes and new ones. His catalog of original compositions for instrumental groups, large and small, continued to grow, as did his collection of distinguished contributions to the popular-song genre. His interest in writing for the stage persisted as well. But a deepening friendship with Marian McPartland inspired a new fascination with piano jazz, manifested in a series of short compositions and one larger one. Still more pivotal was a new attitude of reflection and historical contemplation, both personal and professional, and a commitment to preserve his thoughts for posterity. He had always been a writer, but his yield had often been restricted by the dimensions of a postcard or a page of hotel stationery, his discursive missives to James Sibley Watson notwithstanding. In the early 1970s, he began to expand his literary medium, and his scope, in the direction of a comprehensive memoir. He found that he had a lot of stories to tell and insights to share, not only about himself but also about the music that stood at the core of his artistic consciousness.

American Popular Song

Friends had often encouraged Wilder to put his memories down on paper, to make a literary record of his seemingly endless reserve of personal narratives, collected during extensive travels and while working his way through the music industry in New York. He had made an initial, modest effort at a memoir, called "The Tuxedo," in the early 1960s, and this eventually served as a springboard for more expansive accountings, *The Search* and *Life Story*, in the early 1970s.[1] A few years later, he used material from all of these sources to produce an autobiography in the form of a series of "letters" addressed to key figures in his life; *Letters I Never Mailed* was published in 1975.[2] And in 1976, some of the material emerged again in a never-published memoir about his experiences at the Algonquin Hotel, *Elegant Refuge*.[3]

What may have inspired all of these literary enterprises was a monumental project that Wilder had begun in 1967 with financial support from Jerome Hill's Avon Foundation and that culminated in the first major treatise on popular music, *American Popular Song: The Great Innovators, 1900–1950*, published by Oxford University Press in 1972.[4] Working with the writer James Maher, who served as editor, sounding board, and taskmaster, Wilder initially examined approximately seventeen thousand published songs from the first half of the twentieth century, searching for style features and aspects of originality. He eventually singled out around eight hundred songs for discussion in the book, either in a brief reference or in more extensive analytical commentary, many accompanied by musically notated excerpts. His comments are incisive and authoritative, giving detailed attention to songwriters' methods and artistic essences. He manages to penetrate deeply into a song's secrets without being overly technical or recondite. He is equally perceptive when a song, especially a well-known song, falls short of his high expectations. His colorful personality, self-assured and opinionated, bursts forth vividly from every page. The book offers a valuable historical perspective on a major body of music, boldly fulfilling Wilder's ambition to "lend some patina of dignity and recognition to a unique art form" (*Life Story*, 175).

American Popular Song begins with an introductory chapter on the American song tradition in the late nineteenth century through the First World War, encompassing Stephen Foster, ragtime, and blues, and especially the influence of African music and culture. After that are separate chapters devoted to the six principal figures: Jerome Kern, Irving Berlin, George Gershwin, Richard Rodgers, Cole Porter, and Harold Arlen. Wilder pinpoints each writer's singularity and significance: Kern was a gifted melodist who began the process of breaking free from European roots; Berlin was ingeniously adaptable to circumstances, equally comfortable in theatrical and popular realms; Gershwin brought the language of jazz into the song tradition; Rodgers, especially in his collaborations with Hart, was Kern's equal as a melodist but employed imaginative harmonic structures with comparable brilliance; Porter's lyrics attract immediate attention, but his music is likewise elegant and witty; Arlen, a special favorite, was the first to break completely free from European ancestry, the first to be purely "American." In later chapters Wilder discusses other important songwriters, in an ordering that implies decreasing significance, beginning with a chapter on Vincent Youmans and Arthur Schwartz, followed by a separate chapter on Burton Lane, Hugh Martin, and Vernon Duke, a chapter on ten songwriters who made smaller contributions (Hoagy Carmichael, Walter Donaldson, Harry Warren, Isham Jones, Jimmy McHugh, Duke Ellington, Fred Ahlert, Richard Whiting, Ray Noble, John Green, Rube Bloom, Jimmy Van Heusen), and a final chapter singling out assorted individual songs by others.

Wilder does not spell out his evaluative criteria at the outset of his study but rather demonstrates them gradually, as he discusses song after song of the Big Six. Not until chapter 9, within his commentary on the music of his friend Hugh Martin, does he fully articulate the standards he has been applying:

> I should make clear that my criteria are limited to the singing line and include the elements of intensity, unexpectedness, originality, sinuosity of phrase, clarity, naturalness, control, unclutteredness, sophistication, and honest sentiment. Melodrama, cleverness, contrivance, imitativeness, pretentiousness, aggressiveness, calculatedness, and shallowness may be elements which result in a hit song, but never in a great song. Sometimes one is deceived by devices, in other words, cleverness. The ingenuity implicit in cleverness is as dangerous as are the words of a hollow spellbinder or a beautiful but empty face. (355)

The key to his primary focus lies in the book's subtitle: *The Great Innovators.* What interests him most is cutting-edge originality. The songwriters he likes best are those who surprise him, who move in unexpected directions, perhaps with an unusual harmony or melodic subterfuge. Rodgers "achieved his amazing innovations without resorting to more than an unexpected note here and there, completely startling at first hearing, and ever after a part of one's musical memory" (164). Arlen had the ability to provoke "something resembling an electric shock" (253). Gershwin fares less well; Wilder admires his skill and stylistic flair but finds less that surprises him. "I respect Gershwin," he writes, "but I envy Arlen" (286).

On page after page, Wilder explains exactly what songs do to surprise him. It might be a note in the melody from outside the key: a raised second step near the end of Kern's "Make Believe" ("might as well make be-**lieve** I love you" [59]); a lowered third step in Berlin's "They Say It's Wonderful" (on the word "and" at the end of the bridge [117]); a lowered sixth in Gershwin's "Embraceable You" (the final "my sweet em-**brace**-able you" [150]); a lowered seventh twice in Rodgers's "Isn't It Romantic" ("the oldest magic **word**" and "you were meant for **love**"

[190–91]). The sixth step of the scale in particular, writes Wilder, has a "provocative character" (62), highlighted in songs such as Kern's "Nobody Else but Me" ("thirty-three times" [85]); Berlin's "You're Laughing at Me" (first note of the chorus [112]); Porter's "Let's Do It" ("the most stressed note in the song" [226]); and Hoagy Carmichael's "Skylark" (first note [383]). Surprising harmonies turn up in Kern's "All the Things You Are" (the last chord of the bridge, supporting a melody note that is respelled and reharmonized at the return of the main melody [78]); Rodgers's "Hello, Young Lovers" ("all my good wishes go **with you to**-night" [221]); and Porter's "Ev'ry Time We Say Goodbye" (the second phrase, "ev-ry **time** we say good-bye" [248]). Freshly provocative rhythms stand out in Berlin's "Puttin' on the Ritz" (an "off-balance" stress pattern [104]); Gershwin's "Fascinating Rhythm" (with irregularities that work against a regular harmonic pattern [131]); and Porter's "You Do Something to Me" (an "unexpected rhythmic stunt" at the end of the bridge [227]). Wilder also singles out innovations in formal structure such as melodic connections between a verse and chorus (e.g., Kern's "Ol' Man River" [56]); unusual phrase lengths (e.g., a five-bar phrase in the bridge of Berlin's "Top Hat, White Tie, and Tails" [110]); and novel overall designs (e.g., the ABCD form of Berlin's "The Girl on the Magazine Cover" [98]).

Along the way, Wilder has much to say about features of songs that may not be trailblazing innovations but that are core components of a songwriter's craft. He explains Berlin's use of a two-note "seed" at the beginning of "Cheek to Cheek" (on the word "Heaven") and its subsequent development, "walking up for two measures in a series of imitations" ("and my heart beats so that I can hardly speak" [109–10]). He calls attention to a "harmonically ingenious" chord progression over a chromatic bass line at the beginning of the chorus of Gershwin's "Someone to Watch Over Me" (137). He experiences a "gentle, romantic moment" when the melody of Arlen's "Stormy Weather" falls to the fourth step of the scale ("Don't know why / There's no sun up in the **sky**" [262]). He is impressed by Vernon Duke's adept key mobility in "Autumn in New York": although he believes that unusual key changes within a song can create an air of pretension or overthinking, he is impressed that the "untutored public" has nonetheless "accepted a song as complex as this as an independent popular song" (362).

Wilder also draws valuable conclusions about elements of individuality in each songwriter's work—their signature methods or stylistic fingerprints. A favorite tactic of Rodgers, he explains, was "returning to a series of notes, usually two, while building a design with other notes," as in "The Blue Room" (169), "Bewitched, Bothered, and Bewildered" (169, 216), "Little Girl Blue" (197), "My Funny Valentine" (206), and several other classics. He considers Rodgers the master of "step-wise writing" and of the "adroit use of successive fourths" (174, 192). In Harold Arlen's melodies he notes a preference for the "octave drop," citing examples from "Stormy Weather" (262), "That Old Black Magic" (274), and "Come Rain or Come Shine" (283), among others. He also admires Arlen's harmonic sophistication, which includes signature sounds such as a dominant chord with an added sixth (253, 274). A recurring feature of Gershwin's melodies, notices Wilder, is the repeated note, as in "Embraceable You" (149), the verse of "They Can't Take That Away from Me" (156), "A Foggy Day" (157), and many more. Porter, by contrast, rarely repeats notes but favors chromatic descents, as in the melodies of "Let's Do It" (226), "Night and Day" (231), "All through the Night" (235), "Just One of Those Things" (240), and "I Concentrate on You" (240). Only Irving Berlin escapes tidy characterization: Berlin was the "master of the entire range of popular song" (120), writes Wilder, always adapting his tone and style to circumstances, a "fantastic sponge that absorbed the entire musical world about him and managed to make a seemingly endless and original statement as a result of that absorption" (269).

Wilder occasionally mentions a thoughtful point of cooperation between music and lyrics: the setting of the word "suddenly" in George and Ira Gershwin's "A Foggy Day" (at the end of the last section) is "truly chilling" (158); the harmony of Rodgers and Hart's "I Didn't Know What Time It Was" lacks clarity until the end of the song, supporting the lyric "and I know what time it is now" (213); a lowered sixth-scale step in Porter's "Ev'ry Time We Say Goodbye" ("I wonder **why** a little") is "an expression of loss" (248). For the most part, however, he devotes much less attention to the art of the lyricist. He acknowledges, via his collaborator James Maher's introduction to the book, that the two elements of a song

> cannot be separated. One may talk about *words,* or one may talk about *music,* but one cannot talk about *song* and mean anything less than the combination of the two. . . .
>
> The lyrics of American popular song merit a study equal in scope to this one in order to discover what is unique in their structure, prosody, imagery, rhetoric, diction, rhymes, rhythms, metrics, affective innovations, relation to common speech, their synergistic quality when heard combined with the music of which they are an integral part, and other related characteristics and qualities. (xxvi)

Several reviewers expressed disappointment in the relative inattention to lyrics in Wilder's tome. In Richard Rodney Bennett's view, for example, "any book dealing with the popular song is incomplete if it does not touch on the art of the lyric-writer." Because of this neglect, writes Bennett, Wilder is compelled to "dismiss certain songs which have distinguished lyrics, while joyfully acclaiming others whose lyrics are unsingably awful."[5]

Apart from this issue, however, the critical response to *American Popular Song* was broadly laudatory. Reviewers welcomed a serious treatment of a subject that until then had fallen outside the realm of serious discourse and praised Wilder's informal yet principled writing style and approach. In the *New York Times Book Review* (April 23, 1972), Walter Clemons wrote: "Alec Wilder . . . has done a wonderful thing no one else has thought of: His *American Popular Song* seriously, never solemnly, examines as attentively as if they were Schubert lieder the kind of tunes we whistle every day." The *Times Literary Supplement* (October 27, 1972) described the book as "a notable and overdue contribution to our evaluation of Western music in the twentieth century." Praise poured forth from *Newsweek* (Charles Michener, July 31, 1972), *Stereo Review* (James Goodfriend, July 1972), *Hi-Fidelity/Musical America* (Gene Lees, August 1972), and *Downbeat* (Tom Scanlan, December 7, 1972). The book was one of five recipients of the prestigious ASCAP–Deems Taylor Award, and was also nominated for a National Book Award, one of fourteen in the Arts and Letters category.[6] A book about innovators was itself hailed as a bold innovation. Not since the debut of his octets three decades earlier had Wilder drawn this kind of attention, and in both instances it was for a feat of remarkable originality. Just as he had once brought together instruments and styles not normally found together on the same record, now he had blended the tradition of the scholarly treatise with the subject of popular entertainment.

American Popular Song became Wilder's signature achievement of the 1970s, towering over his other work for the remaining eight years of his life. Evidence of its impact first came in a concert at Philharmonic (soon to be renamed Avery Fisher) Hall in New York in the summer of 1973 sponsored by the Newport Jazz Festival, called "A Jazz Salute to American Song." Festival organizers credited Wilder's book for inspiring an event that was "idea-centered and composer-oriented," by contrast with their more typical "performer-oriented or merely jazz-oriented" programs.[7] Three years after that, in the fall of 1976, came an even greater consequence of Wilder's new celebrity: a series of programs on National Public Radio, called *American Popular Song with Alec Wilder and Friends*, focusing on songs and songwriters and featuring both performances and discussion, at times resembling an audio version of Wilder's book with the musical examples brought to life. Wilder and Loonis McGlohon hosted the programs and welcomed guests such as Tony Bennett, Dick Haymes, Woody Herman, Mabel Mercer, George Shearing, Bobby Short, Marlene VerPlanck, and Margaret Whiting to perform the songs and join the conversation.[8] (McGlohon also accompanied the performers on piano, usually joined by a bassist and drummer.) Each program had a theme, either a particular songwriter or singer or something more offbeat (e.g., "Mildred Bailey and the Band Singers," "The One-Shot Songwriters and Some Inside Songs"), and concluded with a performance of at least one of Wilder's songs, old or new. The series, which was recognized with a Peabody Award in 1977, encompassed twenty-eight programs through April 1977 and then resumed for seven more in 1978 and three more in early 1980.[9] A related concert series at Michael's Pub in New York also played for eight weeks in early 1977, featuring some of the same singers and songs and themes.[10]

One of the goals of the radio series and some of the concerts was to correct an omission often noticed by reviewers: at no point does *American Popular Song* give due consideration to the songs of Alec Wilder. The author was characteristically reluctant to include himself in such a pantheon, even though he surely recognized that he belonged there. In a sense, however, *American Popular Song* is about the songs of Alec Wilder: in highlighting aspects of existing songs that the book's author most cherishes, it draws attention to the features or techniques that he as a songwriter would be most inclined to use. At times he makes this connection himself, as when he writes about the "magic" impact of a tonic chord supporting the second-scale step and then adds, "[E]very time I've been able to use this combination adequately, I've wound up with a good song" (435). In

With Mary Mayo (left) and Mabel Mercer, at a party celebrating the National Public Radio program *American Popular Song* in 1976. (*Louis Ouzer*)

his chapter on Kern, he reflects on a time in his own songwriting history when he "had become involved myself in the excitement of lush harmonic patterns" (30). More frequently, however, his personal tastes are simply inherent in general reflections. An offhand remark about "elements I so admire in a great song," for example, reads like a list of essential qualities of his own best work: "unexpectedness, subtlety, wit, inevitability" (147). Commenting about an Arlen song, Wilder writes: "'I Wonder What Became of Me' is another gentle song, one which is more interesting when heard with its very interesting chromatic harmony. The release is a complex melodic line and richly harmonized, but more capable of standing alone. I should say here that melodies like this, which are conceived in terms of harmony, should not be criticized for not being so convincing when isolated" (282). This is essentially a defense of his own songwriting technique, of the importance of harmony for a song's structure and impact, of melodies he wrote that seem to be "conceived in terms of harmony." He holds certain songwriters, especially Arlen, Rodgers, and Kern, in highest esteem in part because he finds in their work the same sort of harmonic orientation.

In any event, the most personal consequence of Wilder's hard work on *American Popular Song* was a renewed dedication to his own popular songwriting. This began during the early research phase of the book in 1968, and it especially flourished starting in 1976, when he and Loonis McGlohon were spending more time together, working on the radio program. Their song "When Yesterday I Loved You" is typical. Its melody is unusual for a pop song, with wide leaps and unpredictable harmonies; Wilder called it "terribly complex" and "difficult."[11] Formally, it begins with three strains in regular phrasing, as if beginning a conventional AABA, expressing a lyric about a love that may or may not last ("I was afraid the moon would fade / And hide you in the night"). The fourth strain begins as if recapitulating A ("When yesterday I loved you / I gave my heart away") but veers away from a routine repetition to set up the happy news that feelings are mutual, announced in a two-phrase extension ("And then to my surprise / You were telling me you'd stay"). After this, the song moves into a new strain entirely, expressing hope for a love that will last. The form is an amalgam of the two standard pop-music standbys, AABA and ABAC:

A When yesterday I loved you,
It was no schoolboy fling
I gave my heart until death do part,
Or at least through most of spring.

A When yesterday I loved you,
My heart beat young and wild,

And in your eyes, all the sweet surprise
Made me once again a child.

B Oh, yesterday I loved you,
And if I held too tight
I was afraid the moon would fade
And hide you in the night.

A' When yesterday I loved you,
I gave my heart away,
But with the morning sun,
I thought you'd kiss and run.
And then to my surprise
You were telling me you'd stay.

C And if my luck holds out, who knows
Perhaps I'll get to say
I love you more tomorrow
Than I loved you yesterday.

Mark Murphy, who sang "When Yesterday I Loved You" on one of the radio programs in 1978, called it a "fantastic song that stretches out into a whole movie."[12] It does have a more expansive, musically sophisticated aura than many of Wilder's earlier pop songs, borrowing tone and gesture from the tradition of the art song.

Essentially all of Wilder's songs from the 1970s display this same sort of convergence of the cultivated and vernacular. This is nothing new: "I'll Be Around" and other earlier pop songs likewise cross traditional boundaries in one way or another. But the practice is more pervasive in the 1970s, more of a consistent aspect of his craft. Having spent so much of his time since the late 1950s composing for instrumental groups in concert halls, and no longer writing commercial music to pay the bills, he is now moving more comfortably across the stylistic spectrum in all his work. Wilder-McGlohon songs from this period, such as "Be a Child," "Blackberry Winter," "Nobody's Home," and "Where's the Child I Used to Hold?" unquestionably fall into the category of "pop song," projecting absolutely conventional song forms (AABA or ABAC) and yet borrowing liberally from the art-song tradition. The tune of "Blackberry Winter," for example, includes unusually rapid rhythms; Teddi King called them "notes that I have never, ever sung in a piece of popular material," just before performing the song on one of the NPR programs.[13] Straight rhythms and phrasing patterns similarly lend a more refined ambience to "Nobody's Home."[14] Another of their efforts, "Saturday's Child," has an unusual form, ABACA, with irregular phrase lengths. This form arose, according to Wilder, because he failed to notice a verse-chorus structure within McGlohon's lyric and set the entire text as one large chorus. Just before a performance of this song by David Allyn on one of the radio programs, McGlohon remarked, "Melodically, I think this is an art song. I think it's one of Alec's greatest melodies."[15]

In a pop song Wilder wrote to a lyric by his friend Rogers Brackett, "The Echoes of My Life," it is the harmony that so strongly evokes the concert hall.[16] As in other types of sophisticated jazz, by the likes of Bill Evans or Marian McPartland, intricate harmonies and weaving chromaticism call to mind Wagnerian practices, or a song by Hugo Wolf (Example 17). The list of Wilder's collaborators during this period must also include the legendary lyricist-songwriter Johnny Mercer, who had added lyrics to two tunes Wilder had given him when they met for an interview during the research phase of *American Popular Song* (*Songs Were Made to Sing*, 22). Wilder probably did not regard these songs, "The Sounds around the House" and "If Someday Comes Ever Again," and this brief collaboration with a master as any sort of validation of his own contributions to the American songwriting tradition, as both sage and practitioner. At the same time, he certainly recognized the importance of song to his own life and career: "I thought there were songs that I loved, that I didn't need to hear anymore. But I *do* need to hear them. It's like trains. I can't get over the sound and smell of a steam locomotive,

Example 17: "The Echoes of My Life," first strain

hearing the whistle in the night. Songs are part of my emotional being. And I'm not ashamed of it at all. I've written half a ton of concert music. It's an entirely different point of view. And yet I go back to songs like I go back to an old friend, to a garden, to a fireplace, to a cat that's come back after being away."[17]

Music for the Stage

Some of Wilder's other work from the 1970s attests to an abiding interest in writing music for dramatic purposes. In early 1973, after learning that Arnold Sundgaard had had a heart attack, Wilder hoped to lift his former collaborator's spirits by returning to a libretto that Sundgaard had written many years earlier. Wilder explained the circumstances in letter to James Sibley Watson in early 1973:

> A friend wrote a very touching, tender libretto called *The Truth about Windmills*. He submitted it to Schirmer's which had published four short operas of ours, but was given short shrift on the grounds that no audience wants to see or hear an opera about old people.
>
> It's a one-act opera about three residents (inmates?) of an old person's home and an eight-year-old girl. I find it very capably written, the best work my friend has done.
>
> Yet I kept putting it aside, knowing the expense of copying the parts and worse, the unlikelihood of its ever being given, even as much as tried out. Naturally I was influenced by all the other pieces which I've never heard.
>
> But then he had a heart attack, a couple of weeks ago. What can one do to help? Books, flowers, desperately cheerful letters? No. So, out of my gloom and notionless head, I concluded I was honor-bound, as a friend, to do the only thing which might cheer him: write the music.
>
> As I've mentioned, my mind has been a musical blank for a long time. Nevertheless, I've jumped in with both feet. The one fortunate aspect of it is that, due to the simple, old-time nature of the libretto, the music must not be sophisticated or dissonant.[18]

Wilder completed the score for *The Truth about Windmills* in early 1973 and helped prepare the premiere of the work in Avon, New York, on October 12 of that year.[19] His description of the music is apt: for a story about simple moments in the lives of elderly friends and a young girl, he sought to generate charm from musical immediacy and accessibility. It is, in other words, a fairly anti-Wilderian conception, rarely offering surprises or journeys along unexpected musical pathways. Reviewing a production of the opera in 1993, Alex Ross described the music as "singularly dull."[20]

At least the project brought Wilder and Sundgaard back together after a long hiatus, and the following year they collaborated again, on *Nobody's Earnest*, an adaptation by Sundgaard of Oscar Wilde's *The Importance of Being Earnest* for the musical theater. Wilder wrote the songs with his friend Ethan Ayer. This play had been a popular source for previous such adaptations, including the musical *Oh, Ernest!* which played for fifty-six performances on Broadway in 1927 (music by Robert Hood Bowers, book and lyrics by Francis DeWill); a 1957 television musical; *Who's Earnest?* which played in expanded form as *Ernest in Love* for 103 performances off-Broadway in 1960 (music by Lee Pockriss, book and lyrics by Anne Croswell); and operas of the same name by the Italian composer Mario Castelnuovo-Tedesco in 1961–62, and by the Scottish composer Erik Chisolm in 1963 (librettos by the composers).[21] But Wilder, Ayer, and Sundgaard apparently were not familiar with any of these predecessors and simply followed Wilde's original play fairly closely, inserting songs at appropriate locations. The music generally has considerably more personality than the *Windmills* score, including a comic song that amusingly captures a character's pomposity ("A Girl Brought Up with the Utmost Care"), a more involved number developing plot and sounding more like a passage from an opera ("Well, to Speak with Perfect Candor"), and a song at the crux of the plot in act 3 that sounds like an homage to Cole Porter ("The Most Important Thing"). Other songs ("Jack in the Country," "On the Day I Lost My Novel") seem to invoke Gilbert and Sullivan, a sensible inspiration in light of the comic entanglements of Wilde's story. *Nobody's Earnest* premiered at the Williamstown Theater Festival in 1974 and has been performed occasionally since.[22] Its fate may have been partially determined by a scathing review of the premiere production from John Simon in *New York* magazine.[23]

Wilder and Sundgaard continued working together in 1975 on *Western Star*, a revision of their earlier musical *The Wind Blows Free*, but eventually turned their attentions to the concert stage for a cantata celebrating the American bicentennial, *Let Freedom Sing*.[24] Wilder also wrote a cantata with Loonis McGlohon during this time, realizing an idea he had discussed with his friend Father Atwell of the church in Avon. *Mountain Boy* tells the story of a Christ figure growing up in Appalachia and dispensing wisdom and goodness.[25] It would be the last of his many compositions for or about children, a successor to *The Churkendoose* (1946), the Golden Records recordings, *A Child's Introduction to the Orchestra* (1954), *Pinocchio* (1957), *Hansel and Gretel* (1958), *Alice in Wonderland* (1958), *Lullabies and Night Songs* (1965), *Children's Plea for Peace* (1968), and *Land of Oz* (1968). Musically, *Mountain Boy* adopts a childlike innocence, with simple harmonies, straightforward storytelling, and no Wilderian surprises. As he celebrated his seventh decade in 1977, he was still writing music for circumstance, still using music to connect with people, forging new friendships and nurturing old ones. The first performances of *Mountain Boy*, on October 4 and 5, 1980, in a church in Rochester, were presented as a memorial to Father Atwell, who had died the previous March.

Instrumental Postludes

Wilder had continued to write instrumental music while he worked on *American Popular Song* in the late 1960s and early 1970s, as he had always shared time between music for the concert hall and music for popular consumption. After the book was finally published in 1972, however, he returned to his production pace of the past decade, adding new entries to his series of Entertainments, quintets, sonatas, and suites (see "Selected Works," section X). As his circle of friends continued to grow, so did his pool of potential advocates and dedicatees.

A series of short piano pieces in the 1970s, for example, grew from a deepening friendship with the acclaimed jazz pianist Marian McPartland. The two had first become acquainted in the 1950s, recalled McPartland in a tribute in *Downbeat* magazine, but became close friends in the early 1970s: "He came to hear my trio at the Rountowner [in Rochester]. He evidently liked what he heard, for he kept coming back night after night. Sometimes he brought faculty members from the Eastman School, or his close friend, photographer Louis Ouzer. One night as he was leaving he said, 'I'm going to write a piece for you—I'll bring it in this week.' I was pleased, but didn't really believe him. I forgot all about it until the next time he showed up at the Rountowner. He airily tossed me a sheet of music, on which was written, 'Jazz Waltz for a Friend—a small present from Alec Wilder.'"[26] This became the first of several short pieces Wilder wrote for McPartland in 1973 and 1974. Each has the character of a pop song with rich jazz harmonies, typical of the chord structurings McPartland herself might use in her rendition of a jazz standard. Indeed, on McPartland's recording of these Wilder pieces, she treats each one as a springboard for improvisation, exactly as she would any of Wilder's (or anyone's) pop songs.[27] The composer did not mind the liberties, according to McPartland, so long as the full composition was presented unadorned at the outset.[28] In short, these piano pieces are essentially an extension of Wilder's songwriting practice, quite unlike his classically conceived piano pieces from the 1960s, which have titles such as "Suite" and "Sonata-Fantasy."[29]

Meanwhile, for other instruments Wilder continued with his furious production pace of the previous decade.[30] Many new works were inspired by new friendships with the trumpeter Robert Levy and musicians affiliated with the Tidewater Music Festival at St. Mary's College in Maryland.[31] He wrote flute pieces for Virginia Nanzetta (e.g., Suite for Unaccompanied Flute, *Answer to a Poem*) and marimba pieces for Gordon Stout (e.g., Sextet for Marimba and Woodwind Quintet). For Levy's Tidewater Brass Quintet he wrote five new brass quintets between 1973 and 1980, the fourth through eighth in his series.[32] In these works,

Wilder is not blazing new trails but reapplying the tools and approaches he had been using in his music for the concert and recital hall since the 1950s. The fourth brass quintet, for example—dedicated to Harvey Phillips but premiered by the Tidewater Brass Quintet in 1973—ends with the further development of a motive first heard in the first movement, tying everything together just as he had in his first woodwind quintet and first horn sonata in 1954 (see chapter 3). Fugatos in the finales of the fifth and eighth brass quintets (1975, 1980) likewise recall a favorite device since he began focusing more on chamber music in the late 1950s. It is reasonable to assume that virtually any of these works feature a Wilderian blend of jazz and classical styles. The use of a jazzy harmony within an otherwise triadic progression, or a bluesy melodic inflection of a motive first heard in straight rhythms, is no longer a novelty or a cause célèbre, just a foundational element of his compositional language, and he employs such techniques with a deft, practiced hand.

At the Tidewater Music Festival in 1972. (*Robert Levy*)

Wilder's music for larger instrumental combinations in the 1970s added to his catalog new solo works for piano (1974), clarinet (1974), tuba (1975), flute (1977), horn (1979), guitar (1980), and trumpet (1980), as well as two new Entertainments and other ensemble works. One of the solo works for horn, *John Barrows* (1979), memorialized his influential, beloved friend, who had died in 1974. A trip across Wilder's stylistic spectrum could start with his Fantasy for Piano and Wind Ensemble, written in 1974 for Marian McPartland and the Duke University Wind Ensemble, which essentially converts the concert band into a giant jazz group—a "big band" indeed. At the other end of the journey might be the Five Love Songs for Horn and Chamber Orchestra, written for Morris Secon in 1979, which draw from the tradition of the classical tone poem, with the usual echoes of Debussy and Poulenc. Somewhere in the center might be the Serenade for Winds, written for Donald Hunsberger and the Eastman Wind Ensemble in 1979, with its intermovement stylistic contrasts. A full consideration of the stylistic elements of such works reveals that the traditional notion of style has lost its utility—that the sound is not easily or productively categorized as one thing or another, just "Wilder."

Sunset

As Wilder's health began to fail in the late 1970s, his drive to create was slowed but not extinguished. After a cancer-ravaged lung was removed in November 1978, followed by a slow recuperation on Grand Cayman Island, he was still able to work for at least another twelve months, writing chamber music and receiving commissions for music for orchestra (from Mitch Miller) and wind ensemble (from Eastman).[33] He was awarded a Guggenheim Fellowship to support compositional projects in April 1980.[34] The premiere of *Mountain Boy* in Rochester in October of that year became a valedictory event, one of his final public appearances. When he died on December 24, in Gainesville, Florida, he left behind several unfinished scores and a vast network of friends and admirers with rich memories, personal and musical.

No long-term friend was more supportive during Wilder's final months than Frank Sinatra, who asked Wilder for a new song for his next album.[35] Happy to oblige, Wilder and McGlohon wrote "A Long Night" and "South—To a Warmer Place," both of which appeared in 1981 on *She Shot Me Down*, Sinatra's penultimate studio album (Reprise FS-2305). During this period Wilder and McGlohon wrote several other songs together as well, including "Where's That Heartache?" and

"Turn Left at Monday." Each of these efforts is evidence of a songwriting team at the top of its game. While the instrumental music of Wilder's later years blends inconspicuously into similar work of the preceding decades, these late songs stand out as some of his finest contributions to the genre. "Where's That Heartache?" for example, is another chromatic feast, bringing techniques of Wagner and Wolf into the realm of the popular song (Example 18).[36] In its opening phrases, for example, descending chromatic lines first emerge within a progression by fifths (supporting "Where's that heartache they said I'd feel"), then in the roots of the chords themselves ("The day you left me for good, for real"). The spirit of innovation and surprise, which Wilder seemed to rediscover when researching and writing *American Popular Song*, endured until the end.

"A Long Night" is an epic *noir* drama, taking a lonely, dark night as a metaphor for existential despair. The night is filled with "dead ends" and bus rides to nowhere and humiliation at the hands of "wheelers and dealers." Daybreak never comes; the only light comes from a "midnight neon glare." Musically, it first unfolds as a conventional ABAC, contrasting the repeated moanings of the title phrase in the A strains with chromatic sighs in B and C:

A A long night, it's a long night,
My friend.
The barrooms and the back streets!
Dead end.

B Sometimes I thought I saw the sunrise
And good times in the air.
It was just another big town
With midnight neon glare.

Example 18: "Where's That Heartache?" mm. 1–4 (original lead sheet plus realization of harmonies)

A A long night, it's a long night,
I know.
The bus rides and the nowhere
To go.

C I've seen what the street corners do
To things like love and dreams.
Seen what the bottle can do
To a man with his hopes and his schemes.

A A long night, what a long night
It has been.
The wheelers and the dealers,
They win.

B/C I've tasted the ninety-proof gin
And chased it away with the blues.
I rarely paid debts that I owed
But I sure have paid my dues.

A' No daylight, just a long night
For me.

After the C strain, however, we hear A again, and then a new strain that is neither B nor C but a little of both, followed by a final abbreviated A. The song has the sweep and elegance—and even some of the melodic and harmonic flavor—of a Harold Arlen song. It is a somber personal statement by a songwriter who had himself known many long nights, with bottles and ninety-proof gin, and it was a perfect vehicle for Sinatra, also in the twilight of his career, whose rendition draws the weight of the world to its shoulders.[37]

"South—To a Warmer Place" is no brighter in tone, relating a familiar tale about promises and dreams all reduced to rubble by a disaffected lover:

A I'd be glad to stay right here with you,
Fact is, that is what I'd planned to do.
But from that cool look on your face,
I think I'll head south to a warmer place.

A Thought I'd given you the best of me,
I'd be glad to share the rest of me.
But there's a chill in your embrace,
I'd better head south to a warmer place.

Cover of sheet music for "A Long Night." (*TRO archive*)

B Seems like yesterday we would kiss and build a fire.
But now it's ten below.
Seems like yesterday nights were warm with love's desire.
But now it feels like snow.

A I don't mind a cold day now and then
But this long deep freeze has done me in,
And it's too late to plead your case,
So, I'm going south to a warmer place.

Its form is utterly conventional, but once again the tune and its harmonic support test boundaries and defy expectations. The music wanders between metaphors of the wayward lover's cold heart ("the cool look on your face," "a chill in your embrace," "ten below," "feels like snow," "this long deep freeze has done me in") and the aching need for warmth and comfort: "I think I'll head south" concluding the first A, "I'd better head south" at the end of the second, and "So, I'm going south" in the song's final phrase. But what exactly is the "warmer place" with such promise of resolution? It must be more than simple escapism or a prospect of new love in a warmer southern climate. Is it an obscure threat of violence? Of suicide? What about the sexual overtones? Wilder's harmonic misdirections savor the ambiguities. Life's mysteries may have been very much on his mind when he wrote this music in late October 1980, not long before his final trip south, to be near his doctor in Florida. He wrote no more after that.

6 The Music of Alec Wilder

An Assessment

IN HISTORIES OF AMERICAN MUSIC in the twentieth century, Alec Wilder has stood just where he wanted to be: in the gaps. While his claims of embracing obscurity never seem completely genuine, he certainly took pleasure in testing the limits of traditional categories and prejudices, writing music that makes us question how and why conventional margins had been defined. "Labels bore me," he wrote (*The Search*, 41). Unfortunately, his self-definition has been an obstacle to a full assessment of his significance and contributions. Having no true home in either jazz or classical spheres, his work has been too readily dismissed or misunderstood in equal measure from different directions.

Fortunately, questions of piety and purity have become quaint relics in an age of pluralism. We can now appreciate Wilder's anticipation of a twenty-first-century culture that celebrates diversity. If he was writing music that was poorly understood by his contemporaries, he was suffering the fate of all original thinkers, exploring obscurities that would later become widely familiar. He was not the only American composer of his era to reach across traditional boundaries—Copland incorporated popular and folk idioms into scores for ballets and films, and Gershwin translated the language of popular song into works for the concert hall and opera house—but he uniquely blended his influences into a language all his own, a true musical melting pot incisively reflecting the culture from which it emerged.

But let us set aside questions of style and classification. How does the music stand up when considered on its own terms? Listeners are often struck by the tunefulness of Wilder's creations, whether a popular song or a concerto or sonata. To Robert Wason, Wilder "simply knew how to write a beautiful tune."[1] For Mark Tucker, Wilder was a "master of the expressive interval."[2] Gunther Schuller has described the "Serenade" theme from the *Jazz Suite* for four horns (1951) as "a melody worthy of an Ellington or a Gershwin, or a Schubert, and arguably one of the most beautiful melodies ever composed in [the twentieth] century."[3] Wilder himself felt that he had a "natural flair for melody," that "tunes have always come easy" (*Life Story*, 42). Indeed, many of his melodies, in music of all types, easily satisfy one of his own standards of measurement in *American Popular Song:* that a good tune should be capable of standing alone, without accompaniment or any other contextualizing factors.

At the same time, Wilder was equally devoted to a melody's harmonic setting. As he explained in *American Popular Song*, some effective melodies are "conceived in terms of harmony" and may not work so well in isolation (282). To his popular songs he brought the harmonic language of late romanticism. To his music for the concert hall he brought the language of jazz harmony. The personality and distinction of his musical language in general are as much determined by his chord constructions and progressions as by the melodies they support.

Wilder aspired in several ways to be more than a skilled melodist. Good melodies alone, he felt, "don't provide an adequate emotional reward" (*Life Story*, 42). This is one reason he invested so much time and passion in the labors of instrumental composition, working with formal structures larger than a thirty-two-bar song. The movements of his sonatas, concertos, and quintets are rich with thematic relations, motivic development, contrapuntal complexity, and intermovement connections. They represent distinguished contributions to the repertoire for all the instruments, including some that have traditionally been underexplored. For students everywhere who work tirelessly in practice rooms and rehearsal studios perfecting their technique and musicianship, and their teachers, Wilder's work is a treasure.

That does not mean, however, that his large instrumental works blaze new trails in formal construction, on a par with the freshness and originality of his harmonic language or stylistic hybridizations. He set out only to master standard instrumental forms, not to revolutionize their conception. In truth, he worked most comfortably within relatively modest frameworks; at heart, to use his own self-description, he was a "miniaturist" (*The Search*, 41). When he did broaden his formal ambitions, as in some works for large ensembles or some movements from the solo sonatas, his music can seem expansive in dimensions but not in substance—as if he has conceived a larger formal structure without also broadening his expressive aims.

The perfect vehicle for his talent and ambitions was a classic miniature of American music, the popular song. His most important contributions to the music of his time were conceived within, or in relation to, this framework. The octets are essentially instrumental songs, perfectly proportioned to fit on one side of a 78-rpm disc. (At least two were reconceived as actual songs, with lyrics by William Engvick.[4]) They do not necessarily conform with standard song forms, but they have melodies and sections that are inspired by the song-form model. This same model lies at the heart of Wilder's actual popular songs, whether written to satisfy a professional commitment or for more personal reasons. He valued innovations, and he was an innovator, but he needed a familiar starting point, a standard from which to deviate. From deviation comes musical surprises, as Wilder explained at length in *American Popular Song* and practiced in his own songwriting. This could be an unexpected chord or phrase extension, a melody that takes an unforeseen turn, or an extra strain that heightens the drama of a lyric.

And yet surprises are not essential to a song's success. Three of his greatest creations—three of the songs for which Alec Wilder has been and will be most remembered—are absolutely conventional, formally, melodically, and harmonically. "I'll Be Around," "It's So Peaceful in the Country," and "Who Can I Turn To?" are classic AABA forms, with uniform phrase lengths and sophisticated but standard harmonic structures. These are great songs not because they challenge us with novelty and innovation but because they realize a classic model so well. In their simple elegance, they seem to communicate directly and immediately with the heart of each listener. If Wilder's sonatas and quintets achieve eminence in the worlds of instrumentalists, these songs resonate beyond the spheres of singers and song enthusiasts into the world at large; they capture a universality of human experience. They fit Wilder's own descriptions of great songs in his treatise on the subject, as when he swoons over Raymond Hubbell's "Poor Butterfly": "There isn't a suggestion of contrivance in this melody. It flows as freely as sometimes a song does from the pen of one who is truly inspired. It sounds as if it had come to the mind of Raymond Hubbell in a single sitting, with not a phrase polished or revised" (*American Popular Song*, 23). Indeed, Wilder once claimed that "I'll Be Around" came to life in exactly that way: "I found the title—just by accident. I looked back in a notebook for something else and I saw that title staring at me.

I just happened to write it down. So I just wrote [the music], I hate to tell you, in about twenty minutes. You're supposed to take much longer if the song's better, but I just fell into it. I wrote the lyric almost as fast."[5] Like any fine artwork, these songs, and others like them in the Wilder canon, seem already to exist in nature, as if they did not need to be humanly "created." They sound "as natural as if [they] had simply happened."[6]

Wilder's songs are also a perfect reflection of his character. They do not require a long-term commitment. Their literal sonic presence is brief, just a few minutes, but they linger in memory long after they are gone. To thumb through a Wilder song collection is to travel to different places, making brief stops along the way, without ever settling down. They are honest, generous, witty, worldly, sophisticated, in impeccable taste. They embody the Jazz Age. They live through good times and bad, triumphs and heartaches, in salons and saloons. They reflect Wilder's own perspective as he looked back on his career toward the end of one of his memoirs (*Life Story*, 164–65): "Thank heaven I haven't kept track of what's been accomplished, cut notches in a success gun, for I might start wondering what in hell I'd been doing all these years. Fortunately, I don't think notchily, so I can say without a quiver of apology or guilt that I've been celebrating life. I needn't repeat how. I've said it over and over."

NOTES

Chapter 1. Awakenings

1. Wilder's principal memoirs are "The Tuxedo," *The Search*, *Life Story*, and *Letters I Never Mailed* (see the "Note on Sources" in the preface). Other important biographical sources are David Demsey and Ronald Prather, with the assistance of Judith Bell, *Alec Wilder: A Bio-Bibliography* (Westport, Conn.: Greenwood, 1993); and Desmond Stone, *Alec Wilder in Spite of Himself* (New York: Oxford University Press, 1996).

2. *The Search*, 13–14; *Life Story*, 8–9.

3. Cecil Forsyth, *Orchestration* (London: Macmillan, 1914).

4. Institute of American Music, University of Rochester, *American Composers' Concerts and Festivals of American Music, 1925–1971, Cumulative Repertoire* (Rochester, N.Y.: Institute of American Music, 1972), 65. Sibley Music Library at Eastman has a score for the six orchestral songs, presumably Hanson's conductor's score from a performance in 1928. No score for the *Symphonic Piece* survives.

5. *The Search*, 66. Wilder did, however, receive a letter from Hanson fairly soon thereafter, in January 1931, offering warm greetings and encouragement to continue composing (Wilder Archive 4, box 2, folder 2). Wilder's struggles with alcohol throughout his life, and his unfortunate behavior while under its influence, are well documented by Stone, *Alec Wilder in Spite of Himself.*

6. The TRO archive contains ink copies of "Feast" (A/10), "The Tale of Mad Brigid" (B/2), "Dirge" (B/3), "Never Seek to Tell Thy Love" (B/4), "Wild Nights" (B/8), "I Hide Myself" (B/16), "Goat Paths" (D/4), and "The Par-Boiled Ape" (B/9).

7. This score survives in the Wilder Archive 1-2, box 8, folder 24. Apparently the concerto was performed some time later, although Wilder did not hear it (*Letters I've Never Mailed*, 114).

8. Will Friedwald, *Sinatra! The Song Is You: A Singer's Art* (New York: Scribner, 1995), 174.

9. Wilder Archive 1-4, box 9, folders 1 and 2.

10. Whitney Balliett, "Alec Wilder: President of the Derriére-Garde," *New Yorker*, July 9, 1973, 42. Wilder specifies the year of his mother's death in *Letters I Never Mailed* (104).

11. Lewis Jacobs, "Experimental Cinema in America (Part 1: 1921–1941)," *Hollywood Quarterly* 3.2 (Winter 1947–48): 111–24; Hildegarde Lasell Watson, *The Edge of the Woods:*

A Memoir (Rochester, N.Y.[?]: Privately published, 1979), 105–11; Lucy Fischer, "The Films of James Sibley Watson Jr., and Melville Webber: A Reconsideration," *Millennium Film Journal* 19 (1987–88): 40–49; Lisa Cartwright, "U.S. Modernism and the Emergence of 'The Right Wing of Film Art': The Films of James Sibley Watson Jr. and Melville Webber," in *Lovers of Cinema: The First American Avant-Garde, 1919–1945*, ed. Jan-Christopher Horak (Madison: University of Wisconsin Press, 1995): 156–79.

12. Watson seems to have kept all (or virtually all) of Wilder's letters (Wilder archive 4, box 2).

13. *The Second Little Show* played at the Royale and Shubert theaters between September 2 and October 25, 1930.

14. Stone, *Alec Wilder in Spite of Himself*, 39–40; *Life Story*, 43.

15. He did still have a small income stream from a trust fund that had been set up by his mother (*The Search*, 78).

16. At least fifteen scores of early songs survive in the TRO Archive and at the New York Public Library for the Performing Arts at Lincoln Center in New York. None of them is dated, but the handwriting and notation are consistent with other datable scores from this period. In a master list accompanying the library holdings, Wilder's longtime collaborator William Engvick (to whom Wilder gave the scores for safekeeping) surmises that these songs were written "before 1939."

17. Stephen Sondheim, *Finishing the Hat: Collected Lyrics (1954–1981), with Attendant Comments, Principles, Heresies, Grudges, Whines, and Anecdotes* (New York: Knopf, 2010), xvii. Sondheim's introduction to this volume of his collected lyrics offers many useful insights into the songwriting process, including ideas presented here.

18. A piano-vocal score for "Time and Tide" resides in the TRO archive. This song is not the same as an instrumental with the same title recorded in 1950 by the Red Norvo Trio. It is also not the same as a later song in the Wilder catalog (dated 1960), for which Wilder reused only the title and wrote a completely new lyric for a tune by Cy Walter.

19. See Demsey and Prather, *Alec Wilder*, 9; Stone, *Alec Wilder In Spite of Himself*, 51. *Thumbs Up!* played for 156 performances at the St. James Theater, from December 27, 1934, to May 11, 1935.

20. Mildred Bailey, Columbia 35626 (78 rpm, 1940); Johnnie Ray with the Four Lads, Columbia 39750 (78 rpm, 1951); Jeri Southern, Decca 27950 (78 rpm, 1952). In his preface to this song in one of his song collections (*Songs Were Made to Sing*, 82), Wilder indicates that he wrote it "along about 1930." It was first copyrighted in 1940.

21. Columbia 36219 (78 rpm, 1941). Wilder remembers writing this song in an Eastman practice room after returning from a drive in the country with a friend (*Songs Were Made to Sing*, 105). It was first copyrighted in 1941.

22. Sarah Vaughan, Musicraft 533 (78 rpm, 1948); Judy Holliday, *Trouble Is a Man*, Columbia CL-1153 (LP, 1958); Ella Fitzgerald, *Sunshine of Your Love*, Prestige PR-7685 (LP, 1969). Peggy Lee first performed the song in concert and on the radio and made a recording of it in 1946 that remained unreleased until 2008 (*The Lost '40s and '50s Capitol Masters*, Collectors' Choice CCM-917-2). See Iván Santiago-Mercado, "The Peggy Lee Bio-Discography and Videography: The Capitol Years, Part 2," January 22, 2012, accessed August 1, 2012, http://www.peggyleediscography.com/capitolee1a.html. The first released

recording was by the Hall Sisters (RCA Victor 20-2386 [1947]). On a radio program in 1977, Wilder indicated that he wrote "Trouble Is a Man" (music and lyrics) "about 1929 . . . for Ethel Waters" (*American Popular Song with Alec Wilder and Friends*, program 23: "The Songs of Johnny Mercer," with guest Margaret Whiting, broadcast March 6, 1977). It was first copyrighted in 1944.

23. *Life Story*, 182. In an earlier explanation of the rule Wilder was not quite as permissive, giving the arranger freedom to alter the harmony only "within reason" ("The Tuxedo," 50).

24. Wilder indicated that he did this arrangement for "the Camel show," apparently referring to *The Camel Caravan*, a comedy-variety show that aired on CBS radio in the 1930s and often featured Benny Goodman and his band. John Dunning, *On the Air: The Encyclopedia of Old-Time Radio* (New York: Oxford University Press, 1998), 132–33.

25. Orrin E. Dunlap Jr. discussed this current "craze" in an article in the *New York Times* on April 10, 1938, under the headline "Swing It, Mr. Bach." See Dick M. Bakker, "John Kirby, 1938–42," *Micrography* 29 (December 1973): 3, and 30 (April 1974): 1; George T. Simon, *The Big Bands*, 4th ed. (New York: Schirmer, 1981), 410–12, 452–56; Gunther Schuller, *The Swing Era: The Development of Jazz, 1930–1945* (New York: Oxford University Press, 1989), 25, 815; Terry Teachout, "Jazz and Classical Music: To the Third Stream and Beyond," in *The Oxford Companion to Jazz*, ed. Bill Kirchner (New York: Oxford University Press, 2000), 343–56; Irwin Chusid, "Raymond Scott: Accidental Music for Animated Mayhem," in *The Cartoon Music Book*, ed. Daniel Goldmark and Yuval Taylor, foreword by Leonard Maltin (Chicago: A Cappella, 2002), 151–60.

Chapter 2. Breakthroughs

1. Richard Severo, "Mitch Miller, Music Executive and TV Host, Dies," *New York Times*, August 2, 2010. Other biographical information on Miller can be found in Desmond Stone, *Alec Wilder in Spite of Himself* (New York: Oxford University Press, 1996), 54–55; and Ted Fox, *In the Groove: The People behind the Music* (New York: St. Martin's, 1986), 25–71.

2. Fox, *In the Groove*, 29.

3. H. Howard Taubman, "New Compositions on Yaddo Program," *New York Times*, September 11, 1938.

4. *Elegant Refuge*, 73–75. Wilder's other accounts of the meeting appear in "The Tuxedo," 31–33; *The Search*, 79; and *Letters I Never Mailed*, 115–16, 118–19. In Mitch Miller's memory, the octets were entirely his idea: "I was playing with Yella Pessl, the harpsichordist; I was playing Bach concerts and Baroque music in 1937, '38. I said to Alec, 'Why don't we use these instruments with the harpsichord, and make a kind of jazz chamber music?'" (qtd. in Fox, *In the Groove*, 31–32). This is one of many instances in which Miller seems a bit too eager to take credit for just about anything.

5. Edgar Jackson, "Alec Wilder Octet," *Gramophone* 17 (April 1939): 486; Björn Englund, "Discography of the Alec Wilder Octet," *Names and Numbers* 52 (January 2010): 26–28. The personnel varied slightly for subsequent recording dates.

6. *Letters I Never Mailed*, 116. Wilder does not explain the jokes.

7. Stone, *Alec Wilder in Spite of Himself*, 56–57.

8. Gunther Schuller, *The Swing Era: The Development of Jazz, 1930–1945* (New York: Oxford University Press, 1989), 475.

9. See Terry Teachout, "Jazz and Classical Music: To the Third Stream and Beyond," in *The Oxford Companion to Jazz*, ed. Bill Kirchner (New York: Oxford University Press, 2000), 343–56; Susan C. Cook, "Flirting with the Vernacular: America in Europe, 1900–45," in *The Cambridge History of Twentieth-Century Music*, ed. Nicholas Cook and Anthony Pople (Cambridge: Cambridge University Press, 2004), 152–85.

10. Sylvia Marlowe, *Bach to Boogie Woogie*, General 4006-4008 (1940); Artie Shaw and the Gramercy Five, "Special Delivery Stomp," Victor 26762 (1940). See Larry Palmer, *Harpsichord in America: A Twentieth-Century Revival* (Bloomington: Indiana University Press, 1989), 157; Edward L. Kottick, *A History of the Harpsichord* (Bloomington: Indiana University Press, 2003), 457. Mitch Miller was responsible for a resurgence of the instrument in popular culture about ten years later, when he was head of the popular division at Columbia Records and engaged Stan Freeman to play harpsichord in Rosemary Clooney's recording of "Come On-a My House" (1951). Freeman also made an entire album of adaptations of popular songs for harpsichord, guitar, bass, and drums (*Come On-a Stan's House*, Columbia CL-6193 [1951]), which included a version of Wilder's song "Who Can I Turn To?"

11. The excerpts shown in Example 3 are transcribed from the original manuscript score (TRO Archive). Wilder apparently refined the piece further during the recording session, resulting in occasional discrepancies between the manuscript and the recording.

12. *Gramophone* 17 (April 1939): 486. The initial release was Brunswick 8294.

13. Whitney Balliett, "Alec Wilder: President of the Derriére-Garde," *New Yorker*, July 9, 1973, 43.

14. H. E. P., "Lounging with the Longhairs," *Downbeat*, July 15, 1942, 15. Wilder reacted to this article in a subsequent issue, responding that he could "write dissonance with the best of them" and he had "scores filed away which nobody will play because they're too radical" (qtd. in Mike Levin, "Alec Wilder Replies to Charges of H. E. P.," *Downbeat*, August 15, 1942, 19).

15. Sigmund Spaeth, "I'll Play These," *Steinway Review of Permanent Music* 2.10 (December 1941): 8.

16. For example, articles on various aspects of Wilder's professional work appeared in the *Los Angeles Daily News* (June 14, 1941), *Newsweek* (July 28, 1941), the *New York World-Telegram* (September 11, 1942), and *Glamour* (January 1943).

17. As Englund explains, the arrangements for Sullivan were released on Victor (26344, 26372) without credit to the backing musicians, who were under contract with Brunswick ("Discography of the Alec Wilder Octet," 27).

18. Ibid.; David Demsey and Ronald Prather, with the assistance of Judith Bell, *Alec Wilder: A Bio-Bibliography* (Westport, Conn.: Greenwood, 1993), 113.

19. See Frances N. Teague, *Shakespeare and the American Popular Stage* (Cambridge: Cambridge University Press, 2006), 124.

20. Sam Irvin, *Kay Thompson: From Funny Face to Eloise* (New York: Simon and Schuster, 2010), 76.

21. Demsey and Prather, *Alec Wilder*, 106. Emanuel Balaban conducted the New Orleans Symphony.

22. Ibid., 31–32.

23. Ibid., 106.

24. C-3978-2, Okeh-6411 (1941); see "Gene Krupa Sessionography (1941)," Gene Krupa Reference Page, accessed August 2, 2012, http://www.gkrp.net/1941.html. Wilder discussed the grammatical issue, and Krupa's "correction," with Barbara Lea and Loonis McGlohon on a radio program in 1976 (*American Popular Song with Alec Wilder and Friends*, program 7: "Lee Wiley and the Jazz Singers," with guest Barbara Lea, broadcast November 14, 1976). Lea remarked: "And I guarantee you that anybody that says '*whom* can I turn to' ain't never gonna find nobody to turn to!"

25. Jo Stafford with the Tommy Dorsey Orchestra, Victor 27701 (1941); Lee Wiley with Orchestra Conducted by Ralph Burns, on the LP *West of the Moon* (RCA LPM-1408 [1956]); Morgana King, on the LP *The Winter of My Discontent* (Ascot ALS-16014 [1964]); Barbara Lea, on the LP *Remembering Lee Wiley*, (Audiophile AP-125 [1978]).

26. Kenny Burrell, on the LP *Guitar Forms*, arranged and conducted by Gil Evans (Verve V6-8612 [1965]); Ellis Larkins, on the LP *Penthouse Hideaway* (Decca DL-8747 [1960]); Keith Jarrett, on the LP *Standards, Vol. 2* (ECM-1289 [1985]).

27. As explained in Stone, *Alec Wilder In Spite of Himself*, 74–75.

28. Fred Waring and His Pennsylvanians, in the 78-rpm collection *Pleasure Time* (Decca-18776 [1946]); Tony Bennett, 78-rpm (Columbia 39449 [1951]); Peggy Lee, 78-rpm (Capitol 1683 [1951]); Perry Como, 45-rpm (RCA 47-4530 [1952]).

29. Mildred Bailey, 78-rpm (Decca 3953 [1941]); Tony Bennett, 45-rpm (Columbia 41-41341 [1959]); Meredith D'Ambrosio, on the LP *Another Time* (Sunnyside SSC-1017D [1986]).

30. *Songs Were Made to Sing*, 86. In 1976, however, he suggested that he wrote the lyric much more quickly (*American Popular Song with Alec Wilder and Friends*, program 5: "Musical Comedy, Tin Pan Alley, and Movie Songs," with guest Thelma Carpenter, broadcast October 31, 1976).

31. *American Popular Song with Alec Wilder and Friends*, program 5: "Musical Comedy, Tin Pan Alley, and Movie Songs," with guest Thelma Carpenter, broadcast October 31, 1976. The recording by the George Shearing Quintet to which Wilder refers (which does indeed include the same wrong melody notes as the Mills Brothers recording) was released in 1951 (MGM-10956).

32. Richard W. Ackelson, *Frank Sinatra: A Complete Recording History of Techniques, Songs, Composers, Lyricists, Arrangers, Sessions, and First-Issue Albums, 1939–1984* (Jefferson, N.C.: McFarland and Co., 1992), 109.

33. See *Songs Were Made to Sing*, 86. These versions first appeared as follows: Mildred Bailey, *A Mildred Bailey Serenade* (Columbia CL-6094 [1950]); Rosemary Clooney, 78 rpm single (Columbia CO-46276 [1951]); Tony Bennett, *The Many Moods of Tony* (Columbia CL-2141/CS-8941 [1964]). Anita Ellis sang her version in a nightclub scene in a film, *The Joe Louis Story* (1953), backed by the Ellis Larkins Trio. All these singers got the melody right.

34. Wilder wrote "Is It Always Like This?" to cheer up Peggy Lee after a heartbreak (*Letters I Never Mailed*, 194). But Lee seems never to have sung the song, and Wilder gave it instead to Mabel Mercer, who made it part of her lounge act and eventually recorded it

(*Midnight at Mabel Mercer's*, Atlantic 1244 [1962]). Lena Horne also released a memorable rendition (MGM-10615 [1950]).

35. Stone, *Alec Wilder in Spite of Himself*, 69.

36. Wilder's letters to Watson (Wilder Archive 4, box 2) are filled with requests for financial assistance, heartfelt gratitude for recent help, and promises to repay. It is not clear whether (or how much) Wilder did in fact pay him back, nor whether Watson considered the payments to be loans or gifts.

37. Wilder Archive 4, box 2, folder 3.

38. Will Friedwald, *Sinatra! The Song is You: A Singer's Art* (New York: Scribner, 1995): 132–35; James Kaplan, *Sinatra: The Voice* (New York: Doubleday, 2010), 175–76.

39. Ackelson, *Frank Sinatra*, 157, 167, 186. Ackelson credits the other six arrangements to Axel Stordahl.

40. Friedwald, *Sinatra!* 176; Wilder, *Life Story*, 184–85. Mitch Miller conducted the orchestra. The song on the A-side was "American Beauty Rose" (Hal David/Redd Evans/Arthur Altman), from an entirely different session (Columbia ET 1-624/78 38809). The Robeson song, "Old School Teacher," was released on V-disc (614A) in 1945.

41. *Life Story*, 84. Mitch Miller claimed credit for putting Sinatra on the podium—and thus on the album cover—as a way of convincing Columbia to support the project. Because of a wartime shortage of shellac, said Miller, the label was scaling back its recordings and pressings and would have been unwilling to support an album of Wilder recordings otherwise. See Friedwald, *Sinatra!* 176; Kaplan, *Sinatra*, 267–70. Wilder believed that Sinatra first had the idea to conduct; see, for example, Barry Ulanov, "Smart Alec," *Metronome* 63.5 (May 1947): 16–17, 41–42.

42. The recordings were issued on three 78-rpm discs in 1946 (Columbia M-637). In 1950 they were released on vinyl along with rereleases of seven of the earlier octet recordings (Columbia ML-4271).

43. *Life Story*, 84. Miller told Will Friedwald that he rehearsed the group beforehand (Friedwald, *Sinatra!* 176). George Avakian, a staff producer who was present at the session, told James Kaplan that Wilder did (Kaplan, *Sinatra*, 268).

44. *Alec Wilder Octet Album*, Vox VSP-301 (78 rpm set, 1947). Reggie Merrill played bass clarinet, and Dick Wolff played harpsichord. The performers on the other instruments were the same as for the 1938–40 sessions (Englund, "Discography of the Alec Wilder Octet," 28). The session also included rerecordings of two earlier octets, "The Children Met the Train" and "A Little Girl Grows Up," which were issued along with the new ones.

45. Mercury 7001 (78 rpm, 1946). *Herman Ermine* was presented in concert on March 22, 1947, at Central Needles Trades High School in New York (*New York Times*, March 22, 1947).

46. The musical was performed on several consecutive evenings as part of the Ramapo Lyric Festival in Suffern, New York (*New York Times*, August 27, 1950). It was directed by Dale Wasserman, later acclaimed as the author of the stage adaptation of *One Flew over the Cuckoo's Nest* (1963) and of the libretto for *Man of La Mancha* (1965), for which he won a Tony Award.

47. Wasserman also directed and spearheaded the workshop performances under the auspices of the National Theater Institute of the Eugene O'Neill Memorial Theater Cen-

ter in Waterford, Connecticut (*New York Times*, November 18, 1975). Demsey and Prather indicate that the revision included six new songs (*Bio-Bibliography*, 94).

48. In a 1970 interview with Arnold Shaw (Wilder Archive 4, box 1, folder 14).

49. Qtd. in Stone, *Alec Wilder in Spite of Himself*, 91.

Chapter 3. Evolutions

1. "John Barrows (1913–1974)," International Horn Society, accessed August 2, 2012, http://www.hornsociety.org/en/ihs-people/honoraries/43-john-barrows-1913–1974.

2. *Life Story*, 102. See also *The Search*, 64, and *Letters I Never Mailed*, 145–46.

3. "I'll Dance You": Eddy Howard and His Orchestra, Mercury 5351 (1949); "Milwaukee": Kitty Kallen, Mercury 5315 (1949); "I'm Headin' West for a Rest": Dick Jurgens and His Orchestra, Columbia 38811 (1950). "Whippa-Whippa-Woo": Sarah Vaughan, orchestra under the direction of Norman Leyden, Columbia 39001 (1950). On the latter recording, Wilder and Barer are credited under the pseudonyms Conrad Miller and William Webster (see wilderworld.podomatic.com).

4. Wilder Archive 4, box 2, folder 4.

5. *Elegant Refuge*, 71–72. Mary Martin was appearing on Broadway in *South Pacific* during this time. Although Wilder remembers the sessions taking place on Sundays, an announcement in the *New York Times* (January 20, 1950) mentions a backers' audition for *The Impossible Forest* at the Algonquin on an upcoming Monday.

6. *Elegant Refuge*, 72; Desmond Stone, *Alec Wilder in Spite of Himself* (New York: Oxford University Press, 1996), 90.

7. *Central Opera Service Bulletin* 15.2 (Winter 1972–73): 30; David Demsey and Ronald Prather, with the assistance of Judith Bell, *Alec Wilder: A Bio-Bibliography* (Westport, Conn.: Greenwood, 1993), 14, 104. Stone indicates that this was a production of the After Dinner Opera Company (*Alec Wilder in Spite of Himself*, 90). A performance of the opera in 1958 is not, however, listed among that company's past productions on its Web site (accessed August 2, 2012, http://www.afterdinneropera.org/ado_past.html).

8. The 1962 performance is listed among past productions on the company's Web site (accessed August 2, 2012, http://www.afterdinneropera.org/ado_past.html). The cease-and-desist letter from Wilder's attorney was dated November 1, 1967 (Wilder Archive 4, box 1, folder 13).

9. Wilder wrote his lawyer that, according to an announcement he had seen, an Emanuael Levenson had "reorganized, transcribed, and added to many of the pages found in this version." He continued: "I have *assigned no* rights to Mr. Barer. He definitely knows where I live. . . . Conceivably, Mr. Barer considers the entire opera his own to do with as he wishes because of the anonymous $1,000.00 and the cost of the piano reduction. I do not know, however, of any sly-booted law which would permit Mr. Barer to obtain the services of Mr. Levenson without my permission" (Wilder Archive 4, box 1, folder 13).

10. Sam Zolotow, "Jazz to Be Basis of New Musical," *New York Times*, March 23, 1955.

11. Arnold Sundgaard, "Writing Folk Opera with Kurt Weill: Portrait of the Librettist as a Silenced Composer," *Dramatists Guild Quarterly* 16 (1980): 28–29.

12. Review of *Sunday Excursion*, *MLA Notes* 10.4 (1953): 672–73.

13. Wilder Archive 4, box 2, folder 4. The letter is dated July 5, 1955.

14. Mary Pickford had starred in the earliest film version of this story in 1919. More recent remakes had starred Janet Gaynor (1931) and Shirley Temple (*Curly Top*, 1935).

15. *Daddy Long Legs* (1955) starred Fred Astaire and Leslie Caron, with a screenplay by Phoebe and Henry Ephron. According to Desmond Stone, the screenwriter first assigned to the film, the one who brought Wilder and Engvick on board, was Frank Taylor. Wilder and Engvick actually worked more directly with Casey Robinson, who had replaced Taylor early on. See Stone, *Alec Wilder in Spite of Himself*, 97.

16. The title phrase and principal idea borrow from the opening lines of Shakespeare's *Richard III*: "Now is the winter of our discontent / Made glorious summer by this sun of York / And all the clouds that lour'd upon our house / In the deep bosom of the ocean buried."

17. *American Popular Song with Alec Wilder and Friends*, program 4: "The Songs of Hugh Martin," with guest Marlene VerPlanck, broadcast October 24, 1976.

18. Marlene VerPlanck chose this song to sing during her first appearance on Wilder's radio program in 1976 (program 4, October 24). She told him, "It's a haunting melody, a very haunting thing. You know, you hear it once, and all of a sudden this thing just keeps going around in your brain. I know it was going around in mine." Jackie Cain and Roy Kral's recording of the song appeared on their album *The Glory of Love* (ABC-Paramount ABC-120 [1956]), Anthony Newley's on *In My Solitude* (RCA LPM-2925 [1964]), Helen Merrill's on *Something Special* (Inner City ICT-1060 [1967]), and Bill Dobbins's on *Cologne* (Fuzzy Music [2005]).

19. *Life Story*, 135; see also *The Search*, 127. These scores are currently housed in the TRO archive. For a listing, see Demsey and Prather, *Alec Wilder*, 95–103.

20. "Rand Smith Heard in Song Program," *New York Times*, April 25, 1948. The Rhys poem was originally titled "Jo's Requiem." Wilder later renamed the setting of the Sandburg poem "Chick Lorimer."

21. Demsey and Prather, *Alec Wilder*, 91.

22. An original cast recording of the songs from *Kittiwake Island* appeared on Blue Pear (BP-1003 [1960]).

23. Only the Wilder-Engvick songs "Here Beside Me" and "The Osteopathy Rag" appeared on the printed program for *Once Over Lightly*. Demsey and Prather indicate that two others, "So Long to All That" and "It's Monogamy," were also part of the show (*Alec Wilder*, 78, 83).

24. Stephen Battaglio, *David Susskind: A Televised Life* (New York: St. Martin's, 2010), 32–33.

25. "Wilder's Friends Don't Know the Fourth of It," *Downbeat*, January 26, 1955. Demsey and Prather list thirty-one titles that might have been part of the Golden series ("Miscellaneous Children's Stories in Song," *Alec Wilder*, 109). Barer wrote the lyrics for most of them; other credited lyricists include Margaret Wise Brown ("Little Fat Policeman") and Ben Ross Berenberg ("Ellie, the Elegant Elephant").

26. See *Elegant Refuge*, 92–96; Stone, *Alec Wilder in Spite of Himself*, 100; Val Holley, *James Dean: The Biography* (New York: St. Martin's, 1995), 83–85, 124–43.

27. In part 2 of the radio program *Remembering Alec Wilder*, broadcast on National Public Radio on April 12, 1981.

28. Hugh Martin, *The Boy Next Door*, foreword by Michael Feinstein (Encinatas, Calif.: Trolley, 2010), 274–76.

29. Columbia CL-1455/CS-8249. In a radio interview in 1971 (Wilder Archive 3-1, box 4, folders 51–53), Wilder explained that he "stretched" the film music into self-contained movements.

30. Radio interview, 1971 (Wilder Archive 3-1, box 4, folders 51–53). Wilder and Engvick also converted "Ragtime Music" into a song, "Jam," about a romance that begins in a traffic jam, that was published in 2007. *Alec Wilder Song Collection: Centennial Edition* (New York: Ludlow Music, 2007), 14–18.

31. Sinatra's recording of "I See It Now" appeared on the album *September of My Years* (Reprise FS-1014 [1965]). Marlene VerPlanck recorded "Remember, My Child" on an all-Wilder album, *Marlene VerPlanck Sings Alec Wilder* (Audiophile AP-218 [1986]). The performance of "I See It Now" by Mel Tormé was first released as a single (CBS AAG 212-2F, rereleased as a bonus track on the CD *That's All* [Sony 65165]). Jackie and Roy recorded the six Wilder/Engvick songs on their album *An Alec Wilder Collection* (Audiophile ACD-257 [1990]), and "Such a Lonely Girl Am I" on *Lovesick* (Verve V-8688 [1966]).

32. *Life Story*, 124–25. Wilder describes his friendship with Finckel in the 1940s and his short-lived gardening obsession in *Life Story*, 116–24. ("I refused two well-paying arranging jobs in New York simply because I wouldn't forego the glorious succession of bloomings.") The romance seems to have survived for several years, even though the woman "possessed not one physical characteristic I was normally attracted by, she was aggressive, non-musical, and, I learned to my sorrow, she profoundly hated men" (*Life Story*, 124). Wilder explicitly avoids mentioning her name in *Life Story* (124, 130), although in a journal he kept in the early 1950s he identifies her as "Shirley" (Wilder Archive 6-1, box 1, folder 7, entries for December 24, 1951; December 25, 1951; January 18, 1952; and January 29, 1952).

33. Wilder Archive 4, box 3, folder 26.

34. Wilder made this recollection in the 1971 radio interview (Wilder Archive 3-1, box 4, folders 51–53).

35. An article about the New Chamber Music Society in the *New York Times* (August 19, 1951) mentions the group's recent premiere of Wilder's Horn Concerto, although it does not give an exact date and does not indicate that Barrows was the soloist. In *Letters I Never Mailed* (142), Wilder indicates that he wrote the piece for Barrows and that it came after the concerto he wrote for Miller. In Demsey and Prather (*Alec Wilder*, 34), the piece is dated 1953.

36. Demsey and Prather, *Alec Wilder*, 34.

37. Radio interview, 1971 (Wilder Archive 3-1, box 4, folders 51–53).

38. Sandburg's letter, dated March 13, 1954, is preserved in the New York Public Library's Alec Wilder Papers, box 1, folder 5. The poet indicates that he had heard the music broadcast on CBS. The dating of this work to 1960 (in Demsey/Prather, *Alec Wilder*, 31) apparently refers to the recording (Golden Crest CR-4026).

39. Gilbert Gigliotti, *A Storied Singer: Frank Sinatra as Literary Conceit* (Westport, Conn.: Greenwood, 2002): 21–32. The other contributors were Jeff Alexander, Elmer Bernstein, Gordon Jenkins, Billy May, André Previn, Nelson Riddle, and Victor Young (Capitol W-735).

40. *New Music of Alec Wilder*, Riverside RLP 12-219 (1956, not 1957 as dated in Demsey and Prather, *Alec Wilder*, 51). Frank Sinatra wrote the liner notes. Wilder also made a series of arrangements of popular songs for Lowe around the same time (Demsey and Prather, *Alec Wilder*, 40).

41. Marian McPartland, "Alec Wilder: The Compleat Composer," *Downbeat*, (October 21, 1976, 16–17, 49. She mistakenly describes "Mama Never Dug This Scene" as one of the octets.

42. *Life Story*, 128, 153; Stone, *Alec Wilder in Spite of Himself*, 127; Amy L. Likar, "The New York Woodwind Quintet: A Continuing Legacy" (D.M.A. dissertation, Ohio State University, 1999), 59–61.

43. *Life Story*, 128; Stone, *Alec Wilder in Spite of Himself*, 126; *Letters I Never Mailed*, 141–42.

44. "Two New Works at WNYC Festival," *New York Times*, February 18, 1954. The concert was part of a Festival of American Music sponsored by (and broadcast on) the radio station WNYC.

45. The published score and parts for the second woodwind quintet incorporate revisions Wilder made some years later, after the first recording by the New York Woodwind Quintet (Golden Crest CRS-4028).

Chapter 4. Loyalties

1. "Rock—Mass Hysteria or Mass Art?" *New York Times*, November 5, 1972. The essay was published alongside a contrary perspective by the rock critic Patrick Carr.

2. Radio interview, 1971 (Wilder Archive 3-1, box 4, folders 51–53). The work by Vincent Persichetti to which Wilder referred was the Symphony No. 6 ("Symphony for Band"), opus 69 (1956).

3. *Life Story*, 169; David Demsey and Ronald Prather, with the assistance of Judith Bell, *Alec Wilder: A Bio-Bibliography* (Westport, Conn.: Greenwood, 1993), 36.

4. Demsey and Prather, *Alec Wilder*, 33. Sims played it again in 1976 with Sarah Caldwell and the Indianapolis Symphony (*New York Times*, December 21, 1976).

5. Amy L. Likar, "The New York Woodwind Quintet: A Continuing Legacy" (D.M.A. dissertation, Ohio State University, 1999), 61.

6. Demsey and Prather, *Alec Wilder*, 53.

7. Golden Crest RE-7031 has Karr performing the suite with the guitarist Frederic Hand, along with music for bass and piano accompanied by Bernard Leighton.

8. Gunther Schuller, "Third Stream," in *The New Grove Dictionary of Jazz*, ed. Barry Kernfeld (New York: St. Martin's, 1994), 1199. See also Mervyn Cooke, "After Swing: Modern Jazz and Its Impact," in *The Cambridge History of Twentieth-Century Music*, ed. Nicholas Cook and Anthony Pople (Cambridge: Cambridge University Press, 2004), 395–417.

9. Radio interview, 1971 (Wilder Archive 3-1, box 4, folders 51–53). There are exceptions: "Suggestion for Bored Dancers" (pieces for Mundell Lowe [1956]) includes an improvised French-horn solo, and the third movement of the Suite for Baritone Saxophone, Horn, and Wind Quintet (originally written for Gerry Mulligan [1966]) has a passage of improvisation for baritone saxophone.

10. These datings are approximate. In some cases they indicate when the last piece in the set was composed, while the earliest one may have been composed several years earlier.

11. John Barrows, preface to *Twenty-Two Duets for Two Horns*, by Alec Wilder (Newton Centre, Mass.: Margun Music, 1968), n.p.

12. Maher made this recollection on the program *Remembering Alec Wilder*, broadcast on National Public Radio in April 1981, shortly after Wilder's death.

13. Glenn Bowen, "The Clarinet in the Chamber Music of Alec Wilder" (D.M.A. dissertation, Eastman School of Music, 1968).

14. *Letters I Never Mailed*, 167. He did, however, write a Small Suite for Violin and Piano (ca. 1960) and a Sonatina for Violin and Piano (undated). See Demsey and Prather, *Alec Wilder*, 64.

15. See Susan C. Cook, "Flirting with the Vernacular: America in Europe, 1900–45," in *The Cambridge History of Twentieth-Century Music*, ed. Nicholas Cook and Anthony Pople (Cambridge: Cambridge University Press, 2004), 152–85.

16. The canon begins in the right hand of the piano, answered after two bars by the left hand, then by tuba two bars after that.

17. Anthony Newley's recording of "You're Free" appeared on his LP *Tony* (Decca LK-4406 [1961]).

18. *Lullabies and Night Songs*, music by Alec Wilder, illustrations by Maurice Sendak, ed. William Engvick (New York: Harper and Row, 1965).

19. DeGaetani sings thirty-eight of the songs on her album, accompanied by Rayburn Wright's often Wilderesque orchestrations for nine-piece chamber ensemble (Caedmon TC-1777 [1985]). Murphy sings twenty-five, supported by piano and accordion (E1 Entertainment 7746 [2009]).

20. The unpublished scores for these art songs are held by the TRO Archive.

21. Percy Seitlin, *Is Anything All Right?* (New York: Grossman, 1969). The character is Halsey Boudreau, a composer-arranger who likes taxis and trains and shows up periodically for brief stays at the house of the main characters, enriching their lives with quirky projects and contests (90–97).

22. Teddi King, *Lovers and Losers*, Audiophile AP-117 (1976; "Lovers and Losers"); Marlene VerPlanck, *Marlene VerPlanck Sings Alec Wilder*, Audiophile AP-218 (1986; "Lovers and Losers"); Jackie and Roy, *An Alec Wilder Collection*, Audiophile ACD-257 (1990; "Walk Pretty"); Wesla Whitfield, *Live in San Francisco*, Landmark LCD-1531-2 (1991; "Photographs"); Wesla Whitfield, *September Songs: Music of Wilder, Weill, and Warren*, Highnote HCD-7114 (2003; "Lovers and Losers").

23. Dick Haymes, *For You, for Me, for Evermore*, Audiophile AP-130 (1976).

24. *American Popular Song with Alec Wilder and Friends*, program 16: "The Songs of George and Ira Gershwin," with guest Dick Haymes, broadcast January 16, 1977.

25. Information about McGlohon comes from Jerry Shinn and Loonis McGlohon, *Loonis! Celebrating a Lyrical Life* (Greenville, N.C.: East Carolina University Foundation, 2004), 123–53.

26. Ibid., 125.

27. Demsey and Prather state that Wilder and McGlohon wrote "more than a hundred" songs together (*Alec Wilder*, 22), although the listing of song titles in their bibliography includes only thirty-seven by Wilder and McGlohon (68–89).

28. Shinn and McGlohon, *Loonis!* 131–34. See also Ray Martin, "Dilapidated Land of Oz Theme Park Glows with Life for Annual Festival," *Raleigh (N.C.) News and Observer*, September 7, 2010, accessed August 14, 2012, http://www.newsobserver.com/2010/09/07/668243/dilapidated-land-of-oz-theme-park.html; and Emerald Mountain Properties homepage, accessed August 14, 2012, http://www.emeraldmtn.com/LandofOz/landofoz.html.

29. A souvenir record album for the Land of Oz show included cast recordings of all these songs plus dance and incidental music. See James E. Cary homepage, accessed August 14, 2012, http://www.jecary.com/oz/oz.html, http://www.jecary.com/oz/earlyoz/ozwebe/photoz109.jpg. Demsey and Prather, (*Alec Wilder*, 83, 91) and Desmond Stone (*Alec Wilder in Spite of Himself* [New York: Oxford University Press, 1996], 146) also associate the Wilder-McGlohon song "Plenty Good Enough for Me" with this project. This song does not, however, appear on the album, or in Shinn and McGlohon's account of the production (*Loonis!* 131–34).

30. In recent years it has been partially restored and has hosted weddings and events and an annual Autumn at Oz party. Martin, "Dilapidated Land of Oz Theme Park Glows with Life for Annual Festival"; Emerald Mountain Properties homepage.

31. The work was also recorded by this same collective, except with Wilder himself providing the narration (Turnabout TVS-34413).

32. Demsey and Prather, *Alec Wilder*, 90. The working title was *Beauty and the Beast* (book and lyrics by Thomas Gray).

Chapter 5. Celebrations

1. A typescript of "The Tuxedo," with Wilder's pencil corrections, resides in the Wilder Archive 5-2, box 2, folder 8. This document is not dated, but in *Life Story* (58–59), which was written in 1971 and 1972, Wilder indicates that he wrote "an account of my life in the music world" called "No Tuxedo" (an alternate title) "ten years or so ago." The handwritten manuscript for *The Search*, dated 1970 by Demsey and Prather, is in series 5-2, box 1, folder 15. *Life Story* survives in a typescript with pencil corrections, series 6-1, box 1, folder 1, dated 1971 and 1972 within the text (75, 98). David Demsey and Ronald Prather, with the assistance of Judith Bell, *Alec Wilder: A Bio-Bibliography* (Westport, Conn.: Greenwood, 1993), 225.

2. Alec Wilder, *Letters I Never Mailed* (Boston: Little, Brown, and Co., 1975). The book has been reprinted, with an introduction and helpful annotations by David Demsey, as *Letters I Never Mailed: Clues to a Life* (Rochester, N.Y.: University of Rochester Press, 2005).

3. Wilder Archive 5-2, box 1, folders 5 and 6. As explained by Desmond Stone, Wilder and the Algonquin management and potential publishers could never agree whether the book should be primarily a history of the hotel or a personal memoir. Desmond Stone, *Alec Wilder in Spite of Himself* (New York: Oxford University Press, 1996), 212–13.

4. Alec Wilder, *American Popular Song: The Great Innovators, 1900–1950*, ed. and intro. James T. Maher (New York: Oxford University Press, 1972). The book was reprinted in 1990 with a new foreword by Gene Lees. Desmond Stone has a valuable account of the origins of the project and its nature and impact in *Alec Wilder in Spite of Himself*, 153–68.

5. Richard Rodney Bennett, "American Song-Writers," *Music and Musicians* 21.4 (December 1972): 47–48.

6. "ASCAP 1973 Deems Taylor Awards," accessed August 14, 2012, http://www.ascap.com/eventsawards/awards/deems_taylor/1973/index.aspx; Eric Pace, "National Book Awards Nominates 109," *New York Times*, March 19, 1973. The winner, announced about a month later, was Arthur M. Wilson's *Diderot*.

7. McCandlish Phillips, "A Jazz Night of Song That Did It by the Book," *New York Times*, July 6, 1973. A concert of this sort became a regular part of the annual festival.

8. Demsey and Prather have a listing of most of the programs in *Alec Wilder*, 231–35. See also John S. Wilson, "Radio: Alec Wilder and the Art of Pop Song," *New York Times*, October 1, 1976. The series was produced by South Carolina Educational Radio and Television Networks, supported by a grant from the National Endowment for the Arts. The network began rebroadcasting the programs in March 2011. See http://www.scetv.org/index.php/radio/information/american_popular_song_with_alec_wilder_and_friends/ (accessed August 14, 2012).

9. Some leftover segments were edited into an additional thirteen programs ("Alec Wilder Revisited") that were broadcast after Wilder's death in 1983 (Demsey and Prather, *Alec Wilder*, 234–35).

10. John S. Wilson, "A Nightclub Offers Songs—and History," *New York Times*, February 4, 1977. The first two installments included both performances and discussion, as in the radio series. Wilder was not in attendance, at least not when the series began; he was said to be "on Grand Cayman Island working on a brass quintet and finishing a flute concerto" (*New York Times*, February 4, 1977).

11. *American Popular Song with Alec Wilder and Friends*, program 30: "The Song Lyrics of Dorothy Fields," with guest Mark Murphy, broadcast February 9, 1978.

12. Ibid.

13. *American Popular Song with Alec Wilder and Friends*, program 9: "Mildred Bailey and the Band Singers," with guest Teddi King, broadcast November 28, 1976.

14. Carrie Smith sang "Nobody's Home" at the end of one of the radio programs in 1977. *American Popular Song with Alec Wilder and Friends*, program 18: "The Songs of Hoagy Carmichael," with guest Carrie Smith, broadcast January 30, 1977.

15. *American Popular Song with Alec Wilder and Friends*, program 8: "The Songs of Harold Arlen," with guest David Allyn, broadcast November 21, 1976.

16. Mabel Mercer featured this song in her album *Echoes of My Life* (double LP, Audiophile AP-161/162 [1976]).

17. Qtd. in John S. Wilson, "Radio: Alec Wilder and the Art of Pop Song," *New York Times*, October 1, 1976.

18. Wilder Archive 4, box 2, folder 6 (letter dated February 3, 1973).

19. The opera was recorded in 1982, about eighteen months after Wilder's death, by Eastman faculty and students (Pantheon PFN 1971).

20. *New York Times*, March 9, 1993. The work was staged by the American Chamber Opera Company at the Marymount Manhattan Theater.

21. The opera by Castelnuovo-Tedesco was premiered on February 22, 1975, in a production by LaGuardia Community College in New York (*New York Times*, February 22, 1975). The website Music Web International lists other musical adaptations of this play in England in the late 1950s: *Found in a Handbag* (1957, music by Allon Bacon, staged at Margate); *Half in Ernest* (1958, music by Vivian Ellis, Coventry); *Ernest in Time, or My Dark*

Gentleman (1958, music by John de Grey, Canterbury); and *Ernest* (1959, music by Malcolm Sircom, Farnham). Philip L. Scowcroft, "Music Inspired by Oscar Wilde," accessed August 14, 2010, http://www.musicweb-international.com/classRev/2001/Dec01/Oscar_Wilde.htm.

22. For example, it was performed at Moravian College in 1984 and at Bucknell University in 2006.

23. John Simon, "Wilde and Woolly," *New York*, August 27, 1973. Simon rejected the whole concept: "A thoroughly verbal and cruel comedy like *The Importance* can only lose by being chopped up and decked out with the kind of lyrics and tunes that make for musical-comedy success, and the stuff of Broadway musicals can only be shown up and exploded by whatever Wildean wit the book might preserve."

24. In an article in the *New York Times* in 1974, a list of projects under development to celebrate the American bicentennial included an adaptation by Wilder of Carl Van Vechten's 1924 novel *The Tattooed Countess*. Raymond Ericson, "A Bounty of Opera for the Bicentennial," *New York Times*, November 17, 1974. No other record of this project survives; perhaps Wilder decided that a cantata, *Let Freedom Sing*, was a more appropriate way to celebrate the occasion.

25. See Stone, *Alec Wilder in Spite of Himself*, 217–18; and Jerry Shinn and Loonis McGlohon, *Loonis! Celebrating a Lyrical Life* (Greenville, N.C.: East Carolina University Foundation, 2004), 141–42.

26. Marian McPartland, "Alec Wilder: The Compleat Composer," *Downbeat*, October 21, 1976, 16–17, 49.

27. *Marian McPartland Plays the Music of Alec Wilder*, Halcyon Hal-109.

28. McPartland, "Alec Wilder," 17.

29. Demsey and Prather, *Alec Wilder*, 65–68. Many of the earlier pieces were written for young students.

30. It was also during this time that Wilder produced what may be his most-heard creations, arrangements of twenty-one Christmas carols for tuba ensemble, fulfilling a request from Harvey Phillips. The arrangements were first performed by a choir of tubas (and tubists) of all sizes in Rockefeller Center on December 22, 1974. Since then, the "TubaChristmas" has become an annual tradition not only in New York but around the world. (See www.tubachristmas.com.)

31. Desmond Stone has a detailed account of Wilder's association with Levy and Tidewater in *Alec Wilder in Spite of Himself*, 180–87.

32. All five were recorded by the Tidewater Brass Quintet on Gold Crest Records. See Demsey and Prather, *Alec Wilder*, 115.

33. Stone, *Alec Wilder in Spite of Himself*, 217.

34. See John Simon Guggenheim Foundation, "All Fellows," accessed August 14, 2012, http://www.gf.org/fellows/all/; "276 to Receive $4.6 Million in Guggenheim Awards," *New York Times*, April 6, 1980. Wilder's health prevented him from accepting the award.

35. According to Desmond Stone, Sinatra had also offered financial support for Wilder's medical care (*Alec Wilder in Spite of Himself*, 221).

36. Eileen Farrell, a Wilder favorite, included "Where's That Heartache?" on her album *Eileen Farrell Sings Alec Wilder* (Reference RR-36 [1990]).

37. The song has also been a favorite of jazz instrumentalists, including David Demsey (*Demsey Plays Wilder*, Golden Crest RE-7109 [1985]), Vic Juris (*Music of Alec Wilder*, Double-Time DTRCD-118 [1996]), and David Liebman (*Lieb Plays Wilder*, Daybreak 75214 [2005]). Just after Sinatra's album came out, the song was also featured in the off-Broadway revue based on Wilder's life and music, *Clues to a Life* (opened February 3, 1982), sung by D'Jamin Bartlett (cast album, Original Cast Records OC-8237 [1982]).

Chapter 6. The Music of Alec Wilder

1. Robert Wason, "Alec Wilder and American Song," liner notes to *Songs of Alec Wilder*, Eastman American Music Series, vol. 10, Albany Records Troy-404 (CD, 2000).

2. Mark Tucker, "Behind the Beat: The Songs of Alec Wilder," *Newsletter of the Institute for Studies in American Music* 17.1 (November 1987): 8.

3. *Alec Wilder (1907–1980): An Introduction to the Man and His Music* (Newton Centre, Mass.: Margun Music, 1991), 5. According to Robert Levy, Schuller contributed this opinion about the "Serenade" theme to a biographical essay that is jointly credited to Schuller, Levy, and Loonis McGlohon (personal communication, August 1, 2011). The opening bars of this piece are given as Example 9 above.

4. Vocal versions of "Such a Tender Night" and "Walking Home in Spring," with lyrics by Engvick, appear in the *Alec Wilder Song Collection, Centennial Edition* (New York: TRO/Ludlow, 2007), 8–10, 11–13. Engvick added the lyrics sometime after the pieces were originally composed.

5. *American Popular Song with Alec Wilder and Friends*, program 5: "Musical Comedy, Tin Pan Alley, and Movie Songs," with guest Thelma Carpenter, broadcast October 31, 1976. As noted in chapter 2, on another occasion Wilder suggested that he labored over the lyric somewhat (*Songs Were Made to Sing*, 86).

6. Wilder used these words at the very end of his book to describe Frank Loesser's "More I Cannot Wish You" from *Guys and Dolls* (*American Popular Song*, 519).

SELECTED WORKS

I. Contents of the Wilder Songbooks (TRO archive)

SONGBOOK A

1. "Song, I Am Tired to Death" (James Stephens)
2. "Peggy Mitchell" (James Stephens)
3. "Mary Hynes" (James Stephens)
4. "Nancy Walsh" (James Stephens)
5. "Mary Ruane" (James Stephens)
6. "Sweet Apple" (James Stephens)
7. "A Woman Is a Branchy Tree" (James Stephens)
8. "Cinquains" (Adelaide Crapsey)
9. "Annabelle Lee" (Edgar Allan Poe)
10. "Feast" (Edna St. Vincent Millay)
11. "Autumn Chant" (Edna St. Vincent Millay)

SONGBOOK B

1. "Wild Swans" (Edna St. Vincent Millay)
2. "The Tale of Mad Brigid" (James Stephens)
3. "Dirge" (James Joyce)
4. "Never Seek to Tell Thy Love" (William Blake)
5. "And It Was Windy Weather" (James Stephens)
6. "Song" (John Keats)
7. "Fairy Song" (John Keats)
8. "Wild Nights" (Emily Dickinson)
9. "I Felt a Funeral in My Brain" (Emily Dickinson)
10. "I Sing" (Emily Dickinson)
11. "Heart" (Emily Dickinson)
12. "My Friend" (Emily Dickinson)
13. "The Petal of a Rose" (James Stephens)

14. "Besides That" (James Stephens)
15. "Love" (Emily Dickinson)
16. "I Hide Myself" (Emily Dickinson)
17. "Have You Got a Brook?" (Emily Dickinson)
18. [untitled]
19. "The Ancient Elf" (James Stephens)

SONGBOOK C

1. "The Holy Time" (James Stephens)
2. "Retreat" (poet unknown)
3. "Hesperus" (James Stephens)

SONGBOOK D

1. "The Pit of Bliss" (James Stephens)
2. "The Merry Music" (James Stephens)
3. "The Watcher" (James Stephens)
4. "Goat Paths" (James Stephens)
5. "Minuette" (James Stephens)
6. "Fifteen Acres" (James Stephens)
7. [complete song without text]
8. "And It Was Windy Weather" (incomplete; see Songbook B/5)
9. "The Par-Boiled Ape" (James Stephens)

II. Recording Sessions of the Alec Wilder Octet, 1938–40

(Source: Björn Englund, "Discography of the Alec Wilder Octet," *Names and Numbers* 52 [January 2010]: 26–28.)

1938

December 19 (ARC Studios, New York)
"A Debutante's Diary"
"Concerning Etchings"
"A Little Girl Grows Up"
"Neurotic Goldfish"

1939

March 31 (World Studios, New York)
"Such a Tender Night"
"Walking Home in Spring"

June 13 (World Studios, New York)
"Sea Fugue Mama"
"It's Silk, Feel It"
"She'll Be Seven in May"
December 28 (World Studios, New York)
"Please Do Not Disturb"
"The House Detective Registers"

1940

July 17 (Columbia Studios, New York)
"Seldom the Sun"
"Her Old Man Was Suspicious"
"The Children Met the Train"
"Pieces of Eight"
August 7 (Columbia Studios, New York)
"His First Long Pants"
"Kindergarten Flower Pageant"
"Dance Man Buys a Farm"
"Bull Fiddle in a China Shop"

III. Wilder's Popular Songs, 1939–44

COLLABORATIONS WITH WILLIAM ENGVICK

1939 "Don't Leave Me"
"It's Over" (written for *Ladies and Gents*)
"A Month in the Country"
"A Season or Two Ago"
"Such a Tender Night" (from the octet)
"Walking Home in Spring" (from the octet)
1941 "Sleep, My Heart"
"Who Can I Turn To?"
1942 "The Bowling Song"
1943 "At the Swing Shift Ball"
"Happy Valley"
"Lullaby"
"Simple as A, B, C"
"Singin' as We Go"
"'Tain't a Fit Night Out"
Written for *Chance of a Ghost* (revision of *Ladies and Gents*):
"Anywhere Else but Here"
"The Osteopathy Rag"

1944 Written for *Don't Look Now* (revision of *Ladies and Gents*):
"Give My Brain to Harvard"
"Here Beside Me"
"I'm So in Love with a Beautiful Girl"
"I'm Starry-Eyed"
"Will I Win—Will I Lose?"

COLLABORATIONS WITH WILLIAM ENGVICK AND MORTY PALITZ

1941 "Moon and Sand"
"J. P. Dooley III"
1943 "While We're Young"

WILDER AS LYRICIST

1940 "Out on a Limb"
1941 "It's So Peaceful in the Country"
1942 "I'll Be Around"
1943 "I Never Saw Her Again"
"Is It Always Like This?"
1944 "Stop That Dancin' up There"

OTHER COLLABORATIONS

1939 "City Night" (lyric by William Engvick, music with Jack Jenney)
1942 "I'm Sleeping Late Today, General" (lyric by Billy Kaye)
1944 "On the Other Side of the Sky" (lyric by Eddie Pola)

IV. Individual Songs by Wilder and Engvick and Some Contemporaneous Recordings, 1952–56

(Sources: David Demsey and Ronald Prather, with the assistance of Judith Bell, *Alec Wilder: A Bio-Bibliography* [Westport, Conn.: Greenwood, 1993], 68–89, 123–39; wilderworld.podomatic.com.)

1952 "Don't Say Love Has Ended" (recording: Johnnie Ray with the Four Lads and Orchestra [Columbia 39814])
"Don't Stop"
"Good for Nothin'" (recording: Rosemary Clooney and Marlene Dietrich [Columbia 39812])
"I Can't Sit Still"
"Love Me (Baby Can't You Love Me)" (recording: Johnnie Ray with the Four Lads and Orchestra [Columbia 39837])
"Time for Love" (recording: Marlene Dietrich [Philips P. B. 291])
"Wish Me Well"
1953 "The Moon Just Winked at Me"
"(They Call Me) Bang-Bang"

1954 "Dig That Crazy Mixed-Up Kid"
"It's Up to You"
"Parker's Lament" (recording: Frank Parker [Columbia 40156])
"Should I Sing Sweet?"
"Your House"
1955 "The First Time We're Alone Again"
1956 "The April Age" (recording: Don Cherry with Percy Faith and His Orchestra [Columbia 40885])4
"Crazy in the Heart" (recording: Peggy Lee [Decca 29834])
"A Heart to Call My Own" (recording: Lisa Kirk with Percy Faith and His Orchestra [Columbia 40688])
"The Lady Sings the Blues" (recording: Cleo Laine and the John Dankworth Orchestra [DRG MRS-502;written for Billie Holiday but never recorded by her])

V. Individual Songs with Lyricists Other than William Engvick and Some Contemporaneous Recordings, 1952–56

(Sources: Demsey and Prather, *Alec Wilder*, 68–89, 123–39; wilderworld.podomatic.com.)

COLLABORATIONS WITH MARSHALL BARER

1952 "Basta" (Jimmy Dorsey and His Orchestra, Columbia 39728)
"Kalamazoo to Timbuktu" (Mitch Miller and the Paulette Sisters, Columbia 39679)
"Summer Is a-Comin' In" (Nat King Cole, Capitol 1994)
1954 "I Don't Want to Go to Bed"
1955 "Rain, Rain (Don't Go 'Way)"
"Cast Your Bread upon the Waters" (Kit Carson with Dick Hyman's Orchestra and Chorus, Capitol 14630)

COLLABORATIONS WITH ARNOLD SUNDGAARD

1952 "Many a Gal Have I Passed By"
"There's Doubt in My Mind" (Fontane Sisters, RCA 47-4776)
1954 "Baggage Room Blues"

COLLABORATIONS WITH NORMAN GIMBEL

1955 "Ain'tcha-cha Comin' Out T-Tonight?" (Jo Stafford with Paul Weston and Orchestra, Columbia 40538)
"A Million Windows and I"
"Love among the Young" (Rosemary Clooney, Columbia 40498)
"How Did It Go Today?"
"Next Time Around"
1956 "The Thief" (Frankie Laine, orchestra conducted by Jimmy Carroll, Columbia 40720)

OTHER COLLABORATIONS

1952 "Tell Me True" (lyric by Arthur Writ and Leo Israel; recording: Jimmy Dorsey and His Orchestra [Columbia 39728])
"You Weren't There" (lyric by Ruth Poll; recording: Nat King Cole [Capitol 1968])
"Low in the Lehigh Valley" (lyric by Jack Lawrence; recording: Paul Weston and His Orchestra [Columbia 39666])
1953 "Summer Rain" (lyric by Fred Hellerman)
1955 "Man in the Gray Flannel Suite" (lyric by Fred Ebb; recording: Jennie Dean with Jimmie Carroll and Orchestra [Bell 1126])
"Never Love a Stranger" (lyric by Edward Eager)
"The Winter of My Discontent" (lyric by Ben Ross Berenberg; recording: Jackie Cain and Roy Kral [ABC-Paramount ABC-120])

WILDER AS LYRICIST

1952 "I Got Big Eyes for You" (Tommy Dorsey and His Orchestra, Decca 82659)
1954 "Never Mind"
"You Wrong Me"
1955 "I'd Do It All Again"

VI. Important Instrumental Compositions, 1950–61

LARGE ENSEMBLE

1951 *Jazz Suite* (four horns, rhythm section)
1954 *Carl Sandburg* Suite
1956 *Blue the Dreamer, Gray the Gaunt*
Pieces for Mundell Lowe
1960 Entertainment #1

SOLOIST WITH ENSEMBLE ACCOMPANIMENT

1950 Oboe Concerto
1951 Horn Concerto #1
1955 *From Dawn to Dusk* (Piano Concerto)
1957 Suite for Flute and Strings
1959 *Effie Suite* (tuba)
1960 Horn Concerto #2

CHAMBER MUSIC

1954 *Fall of the House of Usher* Suite (woodwinds and percussion)
Woodwind Quintet #1
1955 *Alec Wilder Sketches the World's Most Beautiful Girls* (arrangements)
1956 Woodwind Quintet #2
Solo Suite for Woodwind Quintet

1958 *Alice in Wonderland* Suite (woodwinds and percussion)
Woodwind Quintet #3
1959 Brass Quintet #1
Suite for Brass Quintet
Woodwind Quintet #4
Woodwind Quintet #5
1960 Quintet for Horn and String Quartet
Woodwind Quintet #6
1961 Brass Quintet #2

SOLOIST WITH PIANO ACCOMPANIMENT

1954 French Horn Sonata #1
1956 French Horn Suite
1957 French Horn Sonata #2
1959 Tuba Sonata #1
1960 Alto Saxophone Sonata
1961 Double Bass Sonata
Cello Sonata
Flute Sonata #1
Trombone Sonata

VII. Important Compositions for Large Instrumental Groups, 1960–72

WIND ENSEMBLE

1960 Entertainment No. 1
1965 Entertainment No. 3
1969 Entertainment No. 5

ORCHESTRA OR CHAMBER ORCHESTRA

1966 Entertainment No. 2

SOLOIST(S) WITH ORCHESTRA OR CHAMBER ORCHESTRA

1960 Concerto No. 2 for Horn and Chamber Orchestra
1963 Suite for Brass Quintet and Strings
Suite No. 1 for Tenor Saxophone and Strings
1965 Suite for Guitar and Chamber Ensemble
1966 Suite for Horn and Strings
Suite No. 2 for Tenor Saxophone and Strings
1968 Concerto for Tenor Saxophone and Chamber Orchestra
1972 Entertainment No. 4 for Horn and Chamber Orchestra

SOLOIST WITH WIND ENSEMBLE

1963 Air for Horn and Small Wind Ensemble
1966 Concerto for Alto Saxophone and Wind Ensemble
1967 Concerto No. 1 for Trumpet and Wind Ensemble
1968 Concerto for Tuba and Wind Ensemble
1969 Concerto No. 2 for Trumpet/Flugelhorn and Wind Ensemble
1971 Concerto for Euphonium and Wind Orchestra

VIII. Important Compositions for Chamber Ensembles, 1960–72

WOODWINDS

1960 Woodwind Quintet No. 6
1963 Saxophone Quartet
1964 Woodwind Quintet No. 7
1965 Small Suite for Woodwind Quintet
Suite for Four Bassoons
1966 Suite for Oboe and English Horn
Woodwind Quintet No. 8
1967 Suite for Alto and Bass Flutes
1968 Woodwind Quintet No. 10
1969 Suite for Oboe, Clarinet, and Bassoon
Woodwind Quintet No. 9
1971 Woodwind Quintet No. 11

BRASS

1961 Brass Quintet No. 2
1967 Suite for Nineteen Trombones
1968 Suite for Four Horns
Eight Studies for Three Horns
Twenty-Two Duets for Two Horns
1969 Nonet for Brass Ensemble
1970 Brass Quintet No. 3
Suite (Ten Duets) for Tubas
Trio for Brass
1971 Ten Trios for Tubas
Tuba Trio No. 1

MIXED

1960 Quintet for Horn and String Quartet
1966 Suite for Baritone Saxophone, Horn, and Wind Quintet
Suite for Two Guitars
1967 Twelve Duets for Horn and Bassoon
1968 Suite for String Bass and Guitar
Three Pieces for Horn and Violin

1969	Seven Duets for Horn and Bassoon
	Suite for Oboe and Horn
	Suite for Oboe, Horn, and Harp
1971	Suite for Baritone Saxophone, Woodwind Sextet, Bass, and Drums

IX. Important Compositions for Instrumental Soloist(s) with Accompaniment, 1960–72

	Sonatas (w/piano):	Suites (one soloist):	Suites (2+ soloists):
1960	alto saxophone	tuba, piano (No. 1)	
1961	cello		
	double bass		
	flute (No. 1)		
	trombone		
1962			tuba, bass, piano
1963	clarinet	tuba, piano (No. 5)	horn, tuba, piano (No. 1)
	trumpet		
1964		tuba, piano (No. 2)	clarinet, horn, piano
1965	flute (No. 2)		
	viola		
1966		tuba, piano (No. 3)	flute, clarinet, piano
1967		trumpet, piano	
1968	bassoon (No. 1)	double bass, piano	flute, oboe, bass, harpsichord
	bassoon (No. 2)	tuba, piano (No. 4)	
	euphonium		
1969	bass trombone		
	oboe		
1970	horn (No. 3)	flute, harpsichord	
1971		clarinet, piano	horn, tuba, piano (No. 2)
1972			clarinet, bassoon, piano (No. 1)
[?]	English horn		

X. Instrumental Music, 1973–80

PIANO SOLO

1973	"Jazz Waltz for a Friend"
	"Where Are the Good Companions?"
1974	"Chromatic Quest"
	"Homework"
	"Inner Circle"
	"Lullaby for a Lady"
	"Why?"

SOLOIST(S) WITH OR WITHOUT PIANO

1975 Sonata No. 2 for Tuba and Piano
Suite for Unaccompanied Flute
Suite No. 2 for Clarinet, Bassoon, and Piano
Trio for Flute, Cello, and Piano
1976 "Answer to a Poem" [flute and piano]
Trio for Violin, Cello, and Piano
1977 Geiger Suite [solo flute]
Suite No. 1 for Unaccompanied Trumpet
1978 Suite No. 2 for Unaccompanied Trumpet

CHAMBER MUSIC WITHOUT PIANO

1973 Brass Quintet No. 4
Suite for Clarinet Choir
1974 "Moosacaglia" [oboe, bassoon, French horn]
1975 Brass Quintet No. 5
Woodwind Quintet No. 12
1976 Suite for Two Clarinets
1977 Brass Quintet No. 6
Woodwind Quintet No. 13
Suite for Flute and Marimba
Sextet for Marimba and Woodwind Quintet
1978 Brass Quintet No. 7
Suite for Trumpet and Marimba
Suite for Horn and Tuba
1979 Trio for Flute, Clarinet, and Bassoon
1980 Brass Quintet No. 8
Six Duets for Flute and Violin
Suite for Trumpet and Tuba

SOLOIST WITH ORCHESTRA OR WIND ENSEMBLE

1974 Fantasy for Piano and Wind Ensemble
Concerto for Clarinet and Chamber Orchestra
1975 "Elegy for the Whale" [tuba and orchestra]
1977 Concerto for Flute and Chamber Orchestra
1979 Five Love Songs for Horn and Chamber Orchestra
"John Barrows" for French Horn and Chamber Orchestra
1980 Concerto for Guitar and Orchestra
Concerto for Trumpet and Orchestra

LARGE GROUPS

1975 Entertainment No. 6 (orchestra)
Entertainment No. 7 (wind ensemble)
1979 Serenade for Winds (wind ensemble)
1980 Four Sentiments (and an Afterthought) (orchestra)

FOR FURTHER READING

Alec Wilder (1907–1980): An Introduction to the Man and His Music. Compiled and designed by Nancy Zeltsman. Newton Centre, Mass.: Margun Music, 1991. Includes "A Short Biography" by Gunther Schuller, Loonis McGlohon, and Robert Levy (1–5) and reprints of articles listed below by Whitney Balliett (52–66) and Marian McPartland (71–78).

Balliett, Whitney. "Alec Wilder: President of the Derriére-Garde." *New Yorker*, July 9, 1973, 36–40. Reprinted in Whitney Balliett, *Alec Wilder and His Friends* (Boston: Houghton Mifflin, 1974): 177–205; and *Alec Wilder (1907–1980): An Introduction to the Man and His Music.*

Demsey, David. "More Clues to a Life: The Alec Wilder Archive at the Eastman School of Music." *Notes* 46.4 (1990): 919–27.

Demsey, David, and Ronald Prather, with the assistance of Judith Bell. *Alec Wilder: A Bio-Bibliography.* Westport, Conn.: Greenwood, 1993.

McPartland, Marian. "Alec Wilder: The Compleat Composer." *Downbeat*, October 21, 1976, 16–17, 49. Reprinted in *Alec Wilder (1907–1980): An Introduction to the Man and His Music.*

Prather, Ronald E. "The Popular Songs of Alec Wilder." *Musical Quarterly* 74.4 (1990): 521–49.

Stone, Desmond. *Alec Wilder in Spite of Himself: A Life of the Composer.* New York: Oxford University Press, 1996.

Tucker, Mark. "Behind the Beat: The Songs of Alec Wilder." *Newsletter of the Institute for Studies in American Music* 17.1 (November 1987): 8–10.

Wason, Robert. "Alec Wilder and American Song." Liner notes to *Songs of Alec Wilder* (see "Suggested Listening"). Reprinted in *Alec Wilder: Twenty-five Songs for Solo Voice* (New York: TRO Ludlow, Hal Leonard, 2002): 4–6.

Wilder, Alec. *American Popular Song: The Great Innovators, 1900–1950.* Ed. and intro. James T. Maher. 1972; reprint, with a foreword by Gene Lees, New York: Oxford University Press, 1990.

———. *Letters I Never Mailed.* Boston: Little, Brown, and Co., 1975. Reprinted as *Letters I Never Mailed: Clues to a Life.* Annotations by David Demsey. Foreword by Marian McPartland. Rochester, N.Y.: University of Rochester Press, 2005.

SUGGESTED LISTENING

Alec Wilder: Music for Winds and Brass. Lawrence University Wind Ensemble conducted by Robert Levy. Albany Records Troy-763 (CD, 2005).

American Songbook Series: Alec Wilder. Smithsonian Collection of Recordings. Smithsonian RD 048-24 A 24574 (CD, 1995).

An Alec Wilder Collection. Jackie Cain and Roy Kral. Audiophile ACD-257 (CD, 1990).

Another Time. Meredith D'Ambrosio. Sunnyside SSC-1017D (LP, 1986).

Bob's Wilder: Bob Rockwell Five Plays the Music of Alec Wilder. Stunt Records STUCD-03072 (CD, 2003).

Clues to a Life. Original Cast Album. Original Cast OC-8237 (LP, 1982).

Demsey Plays Wilder. David Demsey, soprano, alto, and tenor saxophones. Golden Crest RE-7109 (LP, 1985).

Eileen Farrell Sings Alec Wilder. Reference RR-36 (LP, 1990), RR-36CD (CD, 1990).

Elaine Sings Wilder. Elaine Delmar. Columbia SX-6044 (LP, 1966).

For the Friends of Alec Wilder. Manhattan Chamber Orchestra conducted by Richard Auldon Clark. Newport Classic NPD-85570 (CD, 1994).

Lieb Plays Wilder. Dave Liebman, tenor saxophone and flute. Daybreak CHR-75214 (CD, 2005).

Lullabies and Night Songs. Heidi Grant Murphy, soprano. E1 Entertainment 7746 (CD, 2009).

Lullabies and Night Songs. Jan DeGaetani, soprano; orchestrated and conducted by Rayburn Wright. Caedmon TC-1777 (LP, 1985).

Marian McPartland Plays the Music of Alec Wilder. Halcyon HAL-109 (CD, 1992).

Marlene VerPlanck Sings Alec Wilder. Audiophile AP-218 (LP, 1986).

Music for Horn. David Jolley. Arabesque Z-6665 (CD, 1995).

Music of Alec Wilder. Vic Juris, guitar. Double-Time DTRCD-118 (CD, 1996).

The Music of Alec Wilder Conducted by Frank Sinatra. Amazon.com (mp3 download).

Neurotic Goldfish: Chamber Works of Alec Wilder. Manhattan Chamber Orchestra conducted by Richard Auldon Clark. Kleos Classics KL-5113 (CD, 2001).

Nighthawks: The Complete Music [of Alec Wilder] for Horn and Piano. Thomas Bacon, horn; Phillip Moll, piano. Summit DCD-170 (CD, 1994).

Roland Hanna Plays the Music of Alec Wilder. Roland Hanna, piano. Inner City IC-1072 (LP, 1980).

7 X Wilder. Bob Brookmeyer 4. Verve V-8413 (LP, 1961), Lone Hill Jazz LHJ-10378 (CD, 2011).

Songs of Alec Wilder. Valerie Errante, soprano; Robert Wason, piano. Eastman American Music Series, vol. 10. Albany Records Troy-404 (CD, 2000).

Such a Tender Night: The Music of Alec Wilder. Manhattan Chamber Orchestra conducted by Richard Auldon Clark. Newport Classic 85630 (CD, 1998).

Take a Walk on the Wilder Side. Laurel Zucker, flute. Cantilena Records 66014-2 (CD, 1997).

Wilder Bassoon. Richard Lottridge, bassoon. GM Recordings GM-2056CD (CD, 1998).

The Winter of My Discontent. Morgana King. Ascot ALS-16014 (LP, 1964).

INDEX

Pages with illustrations (musical, lyrical, photographic) are in *italic*.

PHILIP LAMBERT is a professor of music at Baruch College and the Graduate Center of CUNY. His other books include *To Broadway, To Life! The Musical Theater of Bock and Harnick*.

AMERICAN

Composers

Lou Harrison
Leta E. Miller and Fredric Lieberman

John Cage
David Nicholls

Dudley Buck
N. Lee Orr

William Grant Still
Catherine Parsons Smith

Rudolf Friml
William Everett

Elliott Carter
James Wierzbicki

Carla Bley
Amy C. Beal

Christian Wolff
Michael Hicks and Christian Asplund

Robert Ashley
Kyle Gann

Alec Wilder
Philip Lambert

The University of Illinois Press
is a founding member of the
Association of American University Presses.

Designed by Copenhaver Cumpston
Composed in 9.5/13 Janson Text
with Meta display
by Celia Shapland
at the University of Illinois Press
Manufactured by Sheridan Books, Inc.

University of Illinois Press
1325 South Oak Street
Champaign, IL 61820-6903
www.press.uillinois.edu